Pennsylvania College of Technology

Formerly The Williamsport Area Community College

PENNSTATE

1855

Human Rights
and American
Foreign Policy

Recent titles in
Studies in Human Rights
Series Editor: George W. Shepherd, Jr.

The Politics of Race and International Sport: The Case of South Africa
Richard Edward Lapchick

White Wealth and Black Poverty: American Investments in Southern Africa
Barbara Rogers

Anti-Apartheid: Transnational Conflict and Western Policy in the Liberation of South Africa
George W. Shepherd, Jr.

The United States, the United Nations, and Human Rights: The Eleanor Roosevelt and Jimmy Carter Eras
A. Glenn Mower, Jr.

International Cooperation for Social Justice: Global and Regional Protection of Economic/Social Rights
A. Glenn Mower, Jr.

Human Rights and Third World Development
George W. Shepherd, Jr., and Ved P. Nanda, editors

A. GLENN MOWER, JR.

HUMAN RIGHTS AND AMERICAN FOREIGN POLICY

The Carter and Reagan Experiences

Studies in Human Rights, Number 7

GREENWOOD PRESS
New York • Westport, Connecticut • London

Library of Congress Cataloging-in-Publication Data

Mower, A. Glenn (Alfred Glenn)
  Human rights and American foreign policy.

  (Studies in human rights, ISSN 0146-3586 ; no. 7)
  Bibliography: p.
  Includes index.
  1. Human rights.   2. United States—Foreign relations—
1945-   . I. Title. II. Series.
K3240.4.M675 1987   323.4   87-7528
ISBN 0-313-25082-0 (lib. bdg. : alk. paper)

British Library Cataloguing in Publication Data is available.

Library of Congress Catalog Card Number: 87-7528
ISBN: 0-313-25082-0
ISSN: 0146-3586

First published in 1987

Greenwood Press, Inc.
88 Post Road West, Westport, Connecticut 06881

Printed in the United States of America

The paper used in this book complies with the
Permanent Paper Standard issued by the National
Information Standards Organization (Z39.48-1984).

10 9 8 7 6 5 4 3 2 1

Contents

Acknowledgments

The author most gratefully acknowledges the contributions to this study by many individuals who so generously shared their knowledge, experience, and insights. Some have been identified in the book's bibliography; limitations of space, however, make it impossible to list the numerous officials, principally in the State Department but also in the Justice and Treasury departments, and the personnel of private organizations who were the source of so much relevant and valuable material. The author's most sincere appreciation is expressed to all these persons, and to the one whose support and devotion have been life's supreme gift to him: his wife, Anne.

Introduction

The question of human rights has come to occupy a prominent place in international relations, a field that was once dominated by controversies over thrones and territories. This emergence of human rights as an international-relations agenda item is part of a more general process through which quality of human life has joined power in all its varied forms both as a dynamic of world politics and as an issue with which policy makers must deal.

Evidence of the increasing importance of human rights as an international political concern is found, first, in the heavy and expanding volume of international human rights agreements, both general and specific. On the global level, governments have produced fifty-seven covenants, conventions, resolutions, statements of principle, declarations, and codes of conduct within the United Nations (UN). This work at a global level through the UN has had its regional counterpart in instruments originating in the Council of Europe and the Organization of American States, which have given significant impetus to the movement to provide international protection for human rights.

Further testimony to the growing status of this issue in the world community is the expanding roster of organizations, both intergovernmental and private, committed to the promotion and protection of human rights. The UN and its affiliated agencies, such as the International Labor Organization and the United Nations Educational, Scientific, and Cultural Organization (UNESCO), head a list of such intergovernmental bodies, in addition to the well-established regional organizations. The adoption of an African Human Rights Charter suggests that the Organization of African Unity may become another regional organization actively serving the cause of human rights. A long list of private human rights organizations in many nations has appeared since the mid-twentieth century to support this cause.

Again, the prominence of human rights as an international-relations issue is attested by the place it has come to occupy on the agendas of bodies besides the UN whose major concerns are political rather than functional. The prime example is the thirty-five-nation Conference on Security and Cooperation in Europe, as the Final Act of its original meeting in Helsinki in 1975 contained a section dealing with human rights.

Finally, the stature of human rights as an international relations issue is seen in the increasing tendency of governments to incorporate this concern in the substance of their foreign policy. As one State Department official observed, "It is not just the United States that is interested [in human rights]; more countries now have human rights offices in their foreign ministries."[1] In a similar comment, Jerome Shestack, former U.S. representative to the UN's Human Rights Commission, noted, "Many governments have made human rights an integral part of their foreign policy," and cited the Netherlands and Norway as examples.[2]

The Norwegian government's view of the place of human rights in its foreign policy was set forth in a White Paper issued April 22, 1977. This document called attention to the fact that "by tradition, human rights have been understood to constitute an important part of Norwegian foreign policy," reflecting the central place of individual rights in Norwegian society. Then, after acknowledging that the pursuit of a human rights foreign policy could strain Norway's relations with some governments, the White Paper continued, "After having balanced these two considerations against one another, the Government's conclusion is that the work of expanding the protection of human rights should continue to be both an integrated and substantial part of Norwegian foreign policy."[3]

Human rights has also figured in the foreign policy of another Scandinavian country, Sweden, whose government has frequently taken public stands against oppressive situations, resort to terror, and violations of human rights in other countries. Sweden's reply to the charge that such official criticism of rights violations constitutes "unauthorized interference in the internal affairs of other countries" is that it "considers it fully legitimate to help mobilize international opinion against oppression and intolerance." Sweden's concern for human rights is viewed as an element in its commitment to work for international peace: "there is a direct link between the protection of human rights and the preservation of world peace."[4]

In a statement that placed his government among those that give human rights a place in their nations' foreign policy, an official in the Australian government, speaking to a 1985 session of the UN's Commission on Human Rights, asserted this government's "emphasis on human rights," an emphasis that "reflected a clearer and a stronger awareness within our community of the importance of human rights [springing] from Australia's tradition of democratic values and respect for the rule of law." Its concern for human rights led the Australian government to take strong stands on such violations as those in South Africa, Zimbabwe, and Afghanistan.[5]

Another country to give a foreign policy priority to human rights is France, whose position on this matter has been clearly stated:

The advancement and implementation of human rights are fundamental elements of French foreign policy. France has a special interest in seeing that these fundamental principles are more and more widely recognized and that violations, whatever the circumstances, be condemned and cease as soon as possible.

In a move designed to assist its foreign ministry in "this essential task," France in January 1984 acted to revitalize and transform its advisory committee on human rights. Established at the end of World War II, the committee is made up of representatives of nongovernmental agencies, labor unions, and human rights activists. Now under the authority of the minister of foreign affairs, the committee meets regularly with the minister and has a close working relationship with this official. President Mitterand cited a number of tactics that France uses to implement its human rights policy, in an address of April 20, 1985, saying:

May I remind you that, in the name of our country, I have spoken about Professor Sakharov in the Kremlin, about the rights of Palestinians in the Knesset, about the rights of Israel in Damascus, and about the right of self-determination of the peoples of Central America in the Congress in Washington.[6]

Finally, Canada's Ministry of External Affairs has a human rights division, and the high status of this foreign policy component is further indicated by the fact, noted by Cathal J. Nolan, that by 1979 "linking [foreign] aid with human rights considerations was no longer the policy of one party or government; it was a universally accepted parameter of Canadian foreign policy."[7]

The United States has been a leader in this movement to make human rights an integral part of the machinery and substance of foreign policy. This leadership role was assumed during the presidency of Jimmy Carter, whose election in 1976 set the stage for what could well be described as a "quantum leap forward" in the movement to incorporate this issue into this country's foreign policy. Why this movement received such a powerful impetus at this particular time and under this particular occupant of the White House is a question that is explored in the first chapter of this study.

With the replacement of Jimmy Carter by Ronald Reagan in the White House the inevitable question arose: What would this change in administrations mean for the place of human rights in this country's foreign policy? While the existence of human rights legislation, the presence in the State Department of a Human Rights Bureau, and other institutional arrangements seemed to ensure the survival of this foreign policy element, there was no guarantee that an effort would not be made to repeal the relevant laws or, if they remained on the books, that they would be effectively implemented by the incoming administration. Similarly, there was no assurance that the human rights agencies and offices within the administrative establishment would be encouraged or allowed to function at the highest possible level of effectiveness. Finally, since the shaping of foreign policy is primarily an executive prerogative, it was clear that the status of human rights as a foreign policy factor would depend primarily on the new administration's thinking on this subject.

The experience of nearly six years of the Reagan administration—the period of time covered by the present study—provides the basis for some comparisons between this administration and its predecessor on the place human rights has occupied in their foreign policies. From these comparisons some conclusions can be reached concerning the durability of human rights as a component of U.S. foreign policy. This book discusses the background for comparisons between the human rights performances of the two administrations and conclusions concerning their contribution to the cause of human rights through their foreign policies and the extent to which human rights has become an established factor in this country's dealings with other nations.

The major portion of the book is a general survey of the human rights policies of the two administrations. After an opening background chapter, it deals with the conceptual framework within which each administration's human rights policy was formed, the sources of these policies, and the tactics for implementation. The survey is followed by two case studies of South Africa and South Korea, illustrating the approach taken by the two administrations to human rights situations.

Throughout the study, as appropriate, the pros and cons of each administration's human rights policy are presented to indicate the strengths and weaknesses, the positive and negative aspects of each administration's approach. The presence of these counterbalancing considerations enables the reader to arrive at his/her own conclusions concerning the relative merits of the human rights performance of the two administrations, conclusions that may differ from those reached by the author.

Any attempt to compare the human rights foreign policies of the Carter and Reagan administrations must take into account a number of considerations. First, Carter was the pioneer president in the matter of including human rights among the basic factors for foreign policy decisions. As such, he faced problems and obstructions with which the Reagan administration did not have to contend, and he established precedents that made it easier for his successor to build human rights into his foreign policy to the extent that he chose so to do.

Second, the domestic and international contexts within which the Carter administration operated were obviously not the same as those surrounding the Reagan administration. The kinds of domestic and international pressures and the mix of various foreign policy interests were not the same in the two eras. Therefore, it is fruitless to try to compare the human rights action taken or not taken by either president in a particular situation with what the other would presumably have done in the same instance. The only possible valid comparisons are those that focus on (1) the manner and extent to which the human rights factor was given a place in whatever foreign policy steps were taken by the two administrations, and (2) the thought processes characterizing the two administrations as these processes related to the concept of human rights as a foreign policy component.

In comparing the two administrations, it is also important to remember the time factor. Carter had four years in office, but at the time of this writing Reagan was nearing the midpoint of a second term and therefore was in a better position to make adjustments in his human rights policy.

Finally, what follows in this book is in a sense a portrayal of some of the dynamics that affect foreign policy in general and human rights policy in particular, and this can be useful for academic purposes. It is also a window on the nature of two administrations through which it is possible to see something of their priorities and ways of dealing with situations and governments. Again, this study may be of some use to persons who want to argue the superior merits of one or the other of the two administrations as a supporter and defender of human rights. From the author's standpoint, however, the central point and concern of this study is not the two administrations as such, but the staying power of a foreign policy element—human rights—which holds the potential for helping people everywhere to live better lives.

NOTES

1. Interview at the Department of State, October 1984.

2. U.S. Congress, House of Representatives, Committee on Foreign Affairs, *Political Killings by Governments of Their Citizens: Hearings Before the Subcommittee on Human Rights and International Organizations*, 98th Cong., 1st Sess., November 16 and 17, 1983 (Washington, D.C.: U.S. Government Printing Office, 1983), p. 216.

3. Norway, Royal Ministry of Foreign Affairs, *Norway and the International Protection of Human Rights*, Report to the Storting no. 93 (Oslo, Norway, April 22, 1977), pp. 33f.

4. Swedish Institute, *Sweden's Foreign Policy*, Fact Sheets on Sweden (Stockholm: Author 1984).

5. Gareth Evans, *The Australian Approach to Human Rights*, Address to the UN Commission on Human Rights (Geneva, Switzerland: United Nations, 1985).

6. *Human Rights and French Foreign Policy*, Documents from France, vol. 16.85 (Washington, D.C.: French Embassy Press and Information Service, 1985); and Address by President François Mitterand to the 65th Congress of the League for the Rights of Man, Paris, France, April 20, 1985.

7. U.S. Congress, House of Representatives, Committee on Foreign Affairs, *Human Rights and U.S. Foreign Policy: Hearings Before the Subcommittee on International*

Organizations, 96th Cong., 1st Sess., May 2 and 10; June 21; July 12; and August 2, 1979 (Washington, D.C.: U.S. Government Printing Office, 1979), p. 334; and Cathal J. Nolan, "The Influence of Parliament on Human Rights in Canadian Foreign Policy," *Human Rights Quarterly* 7, no. 3 (August 1985): 383.

Background to the Human Rights Foreign Policies of the Carter and Reagan Administrations

The unprecedented place given to human rights in U.S. foreign policy during the presidency of Jimmy Carter was no historical accident. Rather, it was a natural product of two factors: trends and elements in this country's political history, and the personality and character of Jimmy Carter.

Taken together, these two factors provide answers to the question: Why did human rights come to play such an important part in America's foreign policy at this particular time that it became not only a distinguishing feature of the Carter presidency but a foreign policy element that the next administration, Ronald Reagan's, could not ignore? The two background factors to the human rights foreign policies of the Carter and Reagan administrations will be explored in this chapter as a prelude to the comparison in succeeding chapters of how these two administrations handled this aspect of the foreign policy-making process.

TRENDS AND ELEMENTS IN U.S. POLITICAL HISTORY

The historical context for the emergence during Carter's term in office of human rights as a more influential factor in the making of United States foreign policy has both long- and short-range elements.

The Long-Range Background

The emphasis on human rights under the Carter administration can be understood as a stage in a long struggle to give moralism or idealism a more prominent place in the making of American foreign policy, long dominated by realism. Although what constitutes a "realistic" foreign policy is clearly much debated, realism generally means an approach that insists that considerations of national interest should determine policy decisions. "National interest," in turn, is normally defined in terms of the physical security and economic well-being of the nation and its people. The realist regards these objectives as necessary in a world in which all states pursue their own interests, unrestrained by any effective central political authority.

The realist thus perceives the world as a place where "our enemies are concerned only with their own interests and will be influenced only by our unity, might, and will to use force [in the protection of] our interests." *Realpolitik* is therefore seen as "the only proper philosophy for America in foreign affairs. . . . [There is] little promise in any policy not rooted in tough-minded self-interest."[1]

In the kind of world that the realist sees, diplomacy is intended to serve the nation and its interests, defined in terms of security and well-being. To the realist, attempts to use a nation's foreign policy for any other purpose, such as the promotion of abstract principles or efforts to better the condition of humanity in general, are misguided. Such attempts, it is argued, can lead a nation into actions that are wrong-headed because they are inimical to its basic interests.

Behind such efforts, says the realist, is a spirit of crusading messianism that can produce more harm than good. In thus rejecting campaigns undertaken for professedly noble purposes, the realist is one in spirit with England's Benjamin Disraeli, who, in the face of demands that his country take forceful steps to avenge the Turks' massacre of Armenians, responded by saying that he refused to plunge England into a conflict whose casualties would far outnumber those caused by the Turks.

The realist's rejection of an idealistically based foreign policy is also prompted by his belief that the idealist tends to overestimate the impact of values on international political situations and the behavior of governments. The realist, furthermore, sees the idealist as someone who fails to understand the central place of power in the affairs of nations.

Some realists take a different approach to the moralism/realism question by attempting to settle the debate through a linguistic tour de force: redefining the terms to make realism appear to be moralism. One of America's leading realists, Henry A. Kissinger, provided an example of this kind of purposive semantics in his statement that "the pursuit of American power is moral, because it is intended to preserve the world balance of power for the ultimate safety of all free peoples." Typical, too, of his approach is his asking delegates to the UN General Assembly whether "we will have served moral ends if we jeopardize our own security [by such actions as those intended to protect human rights]."[2]

The realist's position has deep roots in America's experience in foreign affairs. One of its earliest and most dramatic manifestations was President Washington's refusal to side actively with revolutionary France in its conflict with England, on the ground that neutrality best served the interests of the still-infant United States. This stance by America's first president exemplified the realism that historians have attributed to this country's Founding Fathers. Thus the writings of Norman A. Graebner refer to:

the automatic preference [of the Founding Fathers] for the analytical [realist] over the ideological approach to foreign policy which was dictated by their fundamental conservatism. They accepted all the assumptions of the great European statesmen from Richelieu to Bismarck concerning the nature of international society. All nations, they agreed, pursued their interests in a universal system of power politics. Beginning with the war for independence, they defined United States interests in specific, not general terms.

Graebner further noted:

[N]otions of prudent diplomatic action continued to guide American foreign policy during the 19th Century, as seen in the consistency of thought from John Adams, Alexander Hamilton, George Washington, and Thomas Jefferson to John Quincy Adams, James Polk, and William Seward. . . . Nowhere was the American conservative tradition, with its limited view of human progress and thus of legitimate national action more apparent than in its application to foreign affairs.

And, in a concluding comment, he observed that "early American democratic idealism did not . . . determine the functional policies of the nation. Without exception, those responsible for American actions abroad condemned those who attempted to identify the national interest with the cause of humanity."[3]

While realism, with its emphasis on national interest as the primary concern of foreign policy, has long held a central place in the thinking of American decision makers, it has not had a monopoly on the policy-making process. The point has been made that, while "the pragmatic pursuit of vital interests explains much of American foreign policy, it doesn't explain it all" because

like the people who compose them, nations have a self-conception to which they are philosophically and emotionally attached. Like people, they betray these basic principles on occasion under the impulse of powerful desires or fears; but unless the self-conception itself changes, the consequences of flouting it will sooner or later be traumatic for the nation and its leaders.[4]

In the case of the United States, the self-conception is a combination of political and legal principles inherited from the Greeks and Romans and the ethical precepts of the Judeo-Christian tradition. These sources have combined to produce a set of values that Americans have come to accept as committing their nation to such principles as justice, equality, freedom, and the supreme worth of the individual.

There is, in other words, an element of moralism in the American political culture that has led Americans to believe in what David P. Forsythe has called "their exceptionalism." Americans have not only accepted this as part of their national character, but over the years some have insisted that the values that make this country distinctive should find expression in its foreign policy.

The American political culture has thus produced a school of idealism that has posed a challenge to the realistic approach to foreign policy making. The resulting tension in this area of American political experience is the inevitable result of the presence of two dynamics that are frequently assumed to be mutually exclusive.

The idealists appeared early in American history, taking a position opposite to that of President Washington on the issue of the French-English conflict. Their argument against Washington's neutrality was based on the belief that the United States should support a country whose philosophy of "liberty, equality, and fraternity" made it ideologically akin to the United States.

The note of idealism in the American political culture found expression in 1864 in the humanitarian concern directed toward the treatment of Maronites and Christians in Lebanon and again in 1906 when President Theodore Roosevelt protested the massacre of Jews in Russia and Armenians in Turkey by the Russian and Turkish governments.[5]

While there was thus an element of moralism in American foreign policy in the first century or so of this country's existence, its impact was lessened by the predominance of realism and by the feeling on the part of at least some of the nation's leaders that the influence of American values should be exerted through example, not overt action. Typical of this latter attitude is the comment by John Quincy Adams, "The United States is the well-wisher to the freedom and independence of all. She is the champion and vindicator only of her own. She will commend the general cause by the countenance of her voice and the benignant sympathy of her example."[6]

As the nineteenth century came to a close, however, idealism began to assume a more prominent place in U.S. foreign policy. During the presidency of William B. McKinley, realists and idealists began to struggle earnestly to control U.S. foreign policy. According to historian Norman Graebner:

under McKinley established American traditions began to falter, largely because of the ease with which the United States achieved such allegedly humanitarian goals as the freedom of Cuba, the acquisition of the Philippines, and the establishment of the Open Door for China.

This trend gathered strength during the presidency of Woodrow Wilson.

The older tradition was shattered as Wilson led an intellectual assault on every assumption that had guided the country's early leaders. In identifying America's purpose with the establishment of a world free of power politics and anchored to the democratic principle of self-determination, Wilson created a vision so grand in terms of American idealism and self-interest and so undemanding in terms of national power that scarcely one American diplomatist who wielded authority after Wilson cared to question the new assumptions.[7]

Influential statesmen followed Wilson, including William E. Borah, Cordell Hull, Arthur Vandenberg, and John Foster Dulles. All, according to Graebner,

denied that diplomacy played a limited and specific role in settling affairs among nations through negotiation and compromise. They regarded diplomacy, rather, as a means of exhorting nations to accept new principles of peaceful change or of condemning aggressors for pursuing goals achievable only within the context of the older principles of power politics.[8]

The moralistic strain in American foreign policy that became increasingly prominent in the twentieth century called for an idealistic approach to policy making, in direct contrast to the realistic. The idealist asserts that:

1. The country's foreign policy should reflect its political, social, and religious beliefs, not its interests as traditionally defined.

2. Realism is sterile and is unable to mobilize the nation's energies by providing the sense of purpose that is so essential if the country's foreign policy is to win and hold the popular support it needs to succeed.

3. The United States cannot be an effective world leader if its foreign policy is governed entirely by considerations of *realpolitik* and thereby creates the impression that its only concern is its own power position.

4. Unless its foreign policy reflects its moral values, this country cannot provide an attractive alternative to the ideologies of its rivals in the world arena.

5. A principled foreign policy can prevent this country from aligning itself with repressive regimes who are inherently unstable because they lack popular support.

Basic to some of these arguments is the thesis that the most realistic foreign policy is actually the one that is founded on idealism. This thesis reverses the one advanced in support of realism: that realism is, in fact, the higher morality. In the book with the instructive title *Power Through Purpose: The Realism of Idealism* the authors seek to find the ground between "the extremes of utopian worldism and realistic nationalism" and assert that the task of the United States is "to generate power through the appeal of the Western tradition." "A great nation," they contend, "endowed with power and forced into leadership can retain its position and secure its values only by making that power the servant of morality."[9]

This, then, is the nature of the idealism that has played an increasingly important role in the formulation of American foreign policy over the years. It is, of course, impossible to say with any degree of certainty just how influential this moralistic strain has been in shaping policy. What cannot be disputed, however, is that this thread of moralism has run through American diplomatic history along with a feeling that U.S. foreign policy should embody and express the values that constitute this nation's philosophical foundation. Consequently, the nation's pre-Carter history can be seen as setting the stage for his campaign for human rights. Carter, in other words, was not injecting an altogether new note into his country's foreign-policy-making process; rather, he was a twentieth-century successor to all who in the spirit of the early nineteenth-century proponents of American support for revolutionary France have argued that this country's foreign policy should be based on higher considerations than those of a narrowly defined national interest. Viewed against this background of American diplomatic history, Carter emerges as a national leader whose unprecedented attempt to give a central place to human rights in U.S. foreign policy was easier because it was in line with an approach that had long been struggling for recognition.

The Short-Range Background

The stage for Carter's emphasis on human rights was set by trends and events not only in the first 150 years of this country's diplomatic history, but also in the era from the 1930s through the Nixon presidency. The decade before World War II saw the rise of fascism in Western Europe and the persecution of Jews in Hitler's Germany. The horrors of the German concentration camps provided a tragic example of what can happen to the people of a country when their government mounts a systematic attack on their basic human rights. The suffering of the victims of Nazi cruelties also stood as a sobering testimony to the need for greater attention to an old principle of international law: the legitimacy of humanitarian intervention.

One response to this need is found in the charter of the international organization that was created at the conclusion of World War II, the United Nations. Under Article 55 of this Charter the UN is committed to the promotion of "universal respect for and observance of human rights and fundamental freedoms for all," and under the next article, all members "pledge themselves to take joint and separate action in cooperation with the Organization for the achievement [of this purpose.]"

As a treaty, the UN Charter provided a sanction and mandate under international law for action by an external power, or powers, when the government of a country embarks on a program of abusing the rights of its citizens. The UN charter, in other words, made human rights a matter of international concern, and by so doing, gave new impetus to the idea that a nation's foreign policy should reflect something more than considerations of national interest as traditionally defined.

In addition to the Nazi persecution of Jews and the subsequent incorporation of human rights in the UN Charter other elements in the period before Carter took office helped pave the way for his emphasis on human rights. Foremost among these were the Vietnam War, Watergate, and the attitude of the Nixon and Ford administrations toward human rights.

As Ernst B. Haas has noted, the post-Vietnam era was one of "disillusionment with the ability of the United States to promote its way of life by force of arms and the exercise of economic power." In a period like this,

> it is understandable that a new administration would seek a moral focus for a foreign policy that eschewed the methods of its predecessor. It is understandable that it would seek to hold out to the American public and other nations an attractive symbol to legitimate foreign policy, free from the stigma of duplicity, domination, and defeat.[10]

The collapse of the Nixon presidency in the wake of Watergate joined the Vietnam experience to create "the trauma of the 1960s and 1970s," a period that inspired many questions: "Was the trauma [of the 1960s and 1970s] now being distilled into fresh and more intense political demands? Were the people looking in a different direction for adequate leadership?"[11] These rhetorical questions suggest a new mood in the United States, and the appearance of "changes in the composite American psyche" that were favorable to the kind of leadership that Carter offered. In announcing his candidacy for the presidency, he said, "It is time to reaffirm and strengthen our ethical and spiritual and political beliefs." The results of the voting in the 1976 primaries appeared to validate the contention that "a substantial element in the United States was trying to get away from materialism, toward a new respect for things that, though intangible, are real."[12]

This changing mood of the American electorate, carrying with it a desire for a new orientation in this country's foreign policy, was at least partly a result of the Nixon-Kissinger approach to policy. As David Forsythe has noted,

> American foreign policy under Nixon and Kissinger was widely perceived as pushing realism to an unrealistic extent, thus setting the stage for the [subsequent] preoccupation with the issue of human rights. Kissinger's enthusiasm for pure realism became so pronounced that not even his lip-service to human rights could save him from crippling attack. He was criticized not only by liberal Democrats in Congress but also by the Republican right wing, both on the ground that he had ignored human rights and morality.[13]

The decades immediately preceding the Carter presidency were thus a period in which a number of factors combined to create a readiness for a new kind of foreign policy that gave a central place to such moralistic principles as respect for human rights. In the early 1970s Congress began to create this new type of policy, expressing its own dissatisfaction with the Nixon-Kissinger approach by passing a series of laws that increasingly called for the elevation of human rights to a prominent place in American foreign policy.[14]

The human rights legislation that Congress adopted provides the final and most tangible explanation for the fact that human rights assumed the high priority position, in policy making, that it did at this particular time: the late 1970s. Because of this Congressional action, Jimmy Carter assumed office under a clear legislative mandate to give a central place to human rights in making policy decisions.

Thus, the emergence of human rights as a major element in U.S. foreign policy under the Carter administration was clearly the result of both long- and short-range background factors. One long-range factor was the thread of idealism running through this country's approach to foreign affairs. Though largely ineffective in the early years of American history, this inclination toward a moralistic approach not only survived but became an increasingly serious challenger to the realism that traditionally dominated American foreign policy. Because of this deep-rooted aspect of this country's foreign policy outlook, Carter's call for a principled policy with a prominent place for human rights struck a familiar chord.

The idealism that had long been seeking foreign policy expression gained new life just before the Carter presidency. The Vietnam War and Watergate plus the Nixon-Kissinger brand of realism had a powerful impact on the way the Americans felt about the handling of their country's public affairs. They combined to create a readiness, if not a demand, for an American foreign policy that would more faithfully embody the values that have long been considered to be the essence and strength of this country.

Jimmy Carter offered precisely this kind of foreign policy to the American citizenry. He could do so because he brought to his candidacy, and then to the White House, a particular value system, and he had already shown that he took it seriously as a guide to personal conduct and public policy. The character of Jimmy Carter thus joined events and trends in American political history to explain why human rights came to occupy such a prominent place in American foreign policy in the late 1970s. What, then, made Jimmy Carter the kind of person he was and enabled him to provide his particular kind of foreign policy leadership? To this question the discussion now turns.

THE CHARACTER OF JIMMY CARTER

While the circumstances of the times—the impact of the immediate and more remote elements in the American political experience—were conducive to a change in the orientation of this nation's foreign policy in the late 1970s, this development could not have occurred without the presence of the second key ingredient to change: appropriate leadership. Jimmy Carter could—and did—fill this role because four factors combined to make him the kind of person he was as he assumed the presidency: (1) a strong conviction that the country's foreign policy should express its moral values, (2) a profound personal religious experience, (3) a clear concept of the relation between religion and politics, and (4) a background of personal and official involvement with human-rights-related issues and situations.

Carter expressed his commitment to a value-based foreign policy in numerous statements during his campaign for the presidency. In December 1974 he declared that he had a dream: "That this country set a standard within the community of nations of courage, compassion, integrity, and dedication to basic human rights and freedoms." Speaking more directly to the issue of what this country's foreign policy should be and of the president's responsibility to represent his country's basic beliefs, he declared on another occasion:

Our foreign policy ought not to be based on military might nor political power nor economic pressure. It ought to be based on the fact that we are right... honest... decent... truthful... and respectful. In other words, that our foreign policy itself accurately represents the character and ideals of the American people. But it doesn't. We have a different standard of ethics and morality as a nation than we have in our own private lives. And that ought to be changed. The President ought to be the spokesman for this country; and when the President speaks, he ought to represent as accurately as he can what our people are. And that's the basis, I believe, on which a successful foreign policy can be based.[15]

These expressions of commitment to a value-based foreign policy were accompanied by criticisms that contemporary American diplomacy betrayed this country's ideals and led to undesirable consequences. Writing in 1976 concerning U.S. foreign policy as it related to such areas as Pakistan, Chile, Cambodia, and Vietnam, he commented that the American government's foreign policy "has not exemplified any commitment to moral principles. Furthermore, each time we have become embroiled in an embarrassing predicament, it has become apparent that our leaders have often departed from the more decent inclinations of the American people."[16]

These comments echoed Carter's remarks to a Democratic Issues Convention in Louisville, Kentucky, in November 1975, when he raised the question whether

in recent years our highest officials have not been too pragmatic, even cynical, and as a consequence have ignored those moral values that have distinguished our own country from other nations around the world.

Our greatest source of strength has always come

from basic priceless values, our belief in the freedom of religion [and of] speech and expression, our belief in human dignity [and] in the principle of simple justice. These principles have made us great, and unless our foreign policy reflects these principles we make a mockery of the celebration of our two hundredth birthday as we look back to the ideals and hopes of those who founded our great country.[17]

While he thus argued for a value-based foreign policy, Carter apparently did not want to appear to be an extremist at this point. In this address to the Louisville Conference he acknowledged that the question of how the United States should proceed in the effort to support human rights around the world was "difficult . . . [and] requires a great deal of balancing between idealism and realism, of our understanding of the world as it is and . . . of the world as it ought to be."[18]

The kind of balanced approach to policy making that Carter asserted to be necessary can be described as the "realism of idealism." As he later wrote:

I was familiar with the widely accepted arguments that we had to choose between idealism and realism, or between morality and the exertion of power; but I rejected those claims. To me, the demonstration of American idealism was a practical and realistic approach to foreign affairs, and moral principles were the best foundation for the exertion of American power and influence.[19]

Carter was apparently convinced that values such as human rights should be placed at the center of his country's foreign policy, not only because this was the right thing to do, but because this kind of policy would best serve the country's interests. More important than the reasoning behind it, however, was the clear evidence that Carter was committed to putting values like human rights at the center of his administration's foreign policy.

Given the emphasis in the Judeo-Christian tradition on the worth of the individual, it is not suprising that a person like Jimmy Carter, deeply concerned with human rights, should also be an intensely religious individual. So marked was the religious aspect of Carter's personality that he would certainly be included in any list of presidential contenders in whose lives religious faith was a central factor.

Jimmy Carter spoke openly and often concerning how important religion and religious practices were to him. Looking back on his years in the White House, he said:

And I prayed a lot—more than ever before in my life—asking God to give me a clear mind, sound judgment, and wisdom in dealing with affairs that could affect the lives of so many people in our own country and around the world. Although I cannot claim that my decisions were always the best ones, prayer was a great help to me. At least, it removed any possibility of timidity or despair as I faced my daily responsibilities.[20]

The religious faith that Carter carried with him into the White House had its beginning when, as he said, he "accepted Jesus into [his] heart" as an eleven-year-old boy and joined the Plains, Georgia, Baptist Church. In 1967 he underwent what he described as a "deeply profound religious experience that changed my life," and this led him subsequently to refer to himself as a "born-again Christian."[21]

Carter, in other words, had what in religious terminology is called a "conversion experience," something, as we are reminded, that is hard for a nonbeliever to understand but in his case, "completed the formation of his adult character." "To ignore its pervasive effects," we are warned, "would be to skip over the experience that [brought] Carter's being together." From this point on in his life, he possessed a self-confidence and optimism that he had hitherto lacked, and these combined to provide a source of the energy with which he pursued the objectives he set for himself as a leader.[22]

The openness with which Carter professed his religious faith inevitably aroused some negative reactions. Commentators asserted that "he couldn't be serious," that his religious stance was "nothing more than a cloak to win the 'God vote', a cover for his political ambition," and that there was a real danger that Carter's religious commitment would so convince him that what he was about to do in any situation was so right that he would refuse to listen to anyone who challenged his position.[23]

The possibility, however, that Carter's religious orientation would have this effect on his approach to problems was considerably lessened, if not eliminated, by his conception of religion and its place in his life as the nation's political leader. He evidently recognized that there were limits to what he could expect his faith to do for him; it could not, for example, serve as a source of clear-cut, definitive solutions to the complex problems he would face as president. It could, however, encourage him to do what he said he would do when he faced the need to make difficult decisions in situations where the nation's welfare was at stake: "ask God for guidance." His faith thus encouraged him to believe that divine guidance was indeed possible, but it also offered a kind of protection against arrogance. As he said, "Because I am a Christian, I feel my limitations more intensely."[24]

This question of the impact of Carter's religious faith on his conduct as president is directly relevant to the thesis that the new importance of human rights in the late 1970s was the result of the convergence of two factors: (1) favorable circumstances resulting from this country's immediate and longer-range experience, and (2) the character of Jimmy Carter, to which his religious faith was such a vital contributor. If, in turn, his openly professed faith really helped him be the kind of person who could give a new orientation to American foreign policy, it is because (1) there were elements in this faith that were conducive to this experience, and (2) Carter himself could find a useful and satisfying way to bring religion and public affairs together.

Jimmy Carter's religious experience would have had a much less direct impact on his approach to public policy issues if it had been the kind that was concerned only with the spiritual welfare of the individual. While this concern is indeed at the center of the evangelical tradition to which his experience belonged, the social dimension is also present. As Kucharsky notes, "Many evangelicals believe that social progress invariably results from truly effective evangelism."

The possibility and presumably the expectation that a person imbued with the evangelical spirit would also have a sense of responsibility for the social conditions under which his fellow humans lived is exemplified in the life of William Wilberforce. Wilberforce was not only an "aggressive evangelist" but also a leader in movements for social betterment. As a member of the British Parliament, he earned a place in history for his effort, successfully concluded in 1807, to end the slave trade. Wilberforce evidently had his counterparts in those American evangelicals who, in the years when Carter came to national recognition, shared a feeling "long latent, that evangelicals should attempt to take a stronger hand in their country's affairs, especially through political avenues."[25]

Because of its social content, then, Jimmy Carter's religious experience could be expected to influence his concept of the kind of president he should be if his campaign was successful, and this, in turn, could be expected to influence his approach to public policy issues. In foreign affairs, this influence would clearly be in the direction of a value-centered policy that would give a central place to an issue like human rights that related directly to the living conditions of the individuals for whom evangelicals have such a strong concern.

In his own effort to link his religious experience with the world of politics in which he moved, Carter was helped by the writings of theologian Reinhold Niebuhr, particularly his classic work, *Moral Man in Immoral Society* (1932). Niebuhr's influence was evidently quite significant; in the words of one study of Carter's life,

If Carter's politics can't be understood apart from his religion, then his religion can't be understood without relating Niebuhr's words to Jimmy Carter's born again experience. Niebuhr showed Carter how to take that sin-dispelling experience into the sin-filled world of politics.

As Niebuhr noted, it is easier for an individual to "be ethical and follow Jesus" in personal living than to do so in a society whose nature is below Christian standards. "But," he also noted, "the Christian cannot withdraw from society and become an ascetic. The stern duty of the Christian is to bring justice, as far as possible, to a sinful world."

While he thus emphasized the Christian's duty to society, Niebuhr was realistic in what he thought could be accomplished by one who sought to follow this line of duty. "The Christian," said Niebuhr, "may not get very far.... Neither rationality or love will lead us to utopia. We must aim not at a perfect society but at something realistic, like limited justice." Niebuhr thus distinguished between injustice in general, and individual, particular inequities. As he saw it, injustice, as a general condition within which humanity lives, cannot be eliminated; but something can and must be done about specific situations where people are treated unjustly.[26]

Niebuhr's brand of realism provided a satisfying link for Carter between the world of religion as he experienced it, and the "real" world of politics within which he would have to function if he succeeded in his campaign for the presidency. For Carter, the conclusion was that "realism tells us that men will practice injustice, but Christian love tells us that they can be uplifted and recalled to their better selves."[27]

It is easy to see how this kind of thinking could lead Carter to be the kind of person who would make human rights a keynote of his foreign policy, a policy based on the premise that, while it could not be expected to create a perfect world in which all persons were treated with dignity, it could at least hold the promise of eliminating or ameliorating particular situations where individuals and groups were victims of oppression.

The fourth factor contributing to the kind of person Jimmy Carter was as he assumed the presidency was his background of personal involvement with human-rights-related issues and situations. One example occurred during his career with the U.S. Navy, when his submarine crew, which included a popular black sailor, refused to attend a British-sponsored party in Nassau because it was a "whites only" affair. Later, as a businessman in Plains, Carter declined an invitation to join an organization of whites established in the wake of the U.S. Supreme Court's decision against segregated schools. Despite a threat to boycott his peanut business unless he joined and the organizers' offer to pay his membership dues, Carter held to his position, saying, "I've got $5.00, and I'd flush it down the toilet before I'd give it to you."

The church in Plains to which Carter belonged provided another opportunity for him to express his belief in racial equality. Carter was a deacon in this church but was not present when the board of deacons took action to bar blacks from services. At the next monthly church conference, however, Carter urged a reversal of the deacons' decision, a proposal that only the Carter family supported.

In 1963 Carter began the first of two terms as a state senator, and he achieved some prominence when he worked on a new state constitution and gave particular attention to another area of civil rights: freedom of religion. As Kucharsky notes, "Carter favored the language of the U.S. Constitution while others called for a more theistic clause."[28]

Carter's career as a Georgia politician saw him move from the state Senate to the governor's mansion. In his inaugural speech he declared: "The time for racial discrimination is over. . . . No . . . black person should ever have to bear the . . . burden of being deprived of the opportunity of an education, a job, or simple justice."[29]

Carter's tenure as governor was marked by substantial progress in race relations, with Carter taking such steps as placing qualified blacks in important positions and adding portraits of outstanding blacks to those of whites that had previously monopolized the galleries of the state office building.

Reflecting a concern for the quality of people's lives that found later expression in his emphasis as president on human rights, Carter gave particular attention to the work of the state's Department of Human Resources. Carter saw this as a place where "the troubled Georgian" could go for relief of such problems as sickness, unemployment, disability, or position as a single parent. Partly because of his interest in the work of this agency, the image of Carter the governor came to include the quality of compassion for the poor and sensitivity to injustice.

Later Carter summed up his political career in Georgia by saying,

By the time my terms as state senator and governor were over, I had gained the trust and political support of some of the great civil rights leaders in my region of the country.[30]

Thus, it is apparent that when Carter entered the White House, he did so from a personal background of experience with the belief that the political process could be used to improve the quality of human life; and this was a belief which, in turn, expressed a deep commitment to the kind of values which are inherent in the Christian faith which he openly professed. Jimmy Carter, in other words, was the kind of person who, by virtue of background and personal value system, could be expected to make human rights a focal point of foreign policy.

NOTES

1. Thomas I. Cook and Malcolm Moos, *Power Through Purpose: The Realism of Idealism* (Baltimore: Johns Hopkins University Press, 1954), p. 118.

2. Henry A. Kissinger, *The White House Years*, (Boston: Little, Brown, 1979), p. 91, and speech of October 17, 1973, at the United Nations, both quoted by David P. Forsythe, *American Foreign Policy in an Uncertain World* (Lincoln, Nebraska: University of Nebraska Press, 1984), p. 267.

3. Norman A. Graebner, *Ideas and Diplomacy: Readings in the Intellectual Tradition of American Foreign Policy*, (New York: Oxford University Press, 1964), p. lx.

4. Norman J. Padelford, George A. Lincoln, and Lee D. Olvey, *The Dynamics of International Politics*, 3d ed. (New York: Macmillan, 1976), p. 260.

5. U.S. Congress, House of Representatives, Committee on Foreign Affairs, *Review of U.S. Human Rights Policy: Hearings Before the Subcommittee on Human Rights and International Organizations*, 98th Cong., 1st Sess., March 3; June 28; September 21, 1983 (Washington, D.C.: U.S. Government Printing Office, 1983), p. 35.

6. Forsythe, *American Foreign Policy*, p. 268.

7. Graebner, *Ideas and Diplomacy*, p. lx.

8. Ibid.

9. Cook and Moos, *Power Through Purpose*, pp. 33, 155.

10. Kenneth A. Oye, Donald Rothchild, and Robert J. Lieber, eds. *Eagle Entangled: U.S. Foreign Policy in a Complex World* (New York: Longman, 1979), p. 168.

11. David Kucharsky, *The Man from Plains* (New York: Harper and Row, 1976), p. 7.

12. Ibid., pp. 7, 87, 120.

13. Forsythe, *American Foreign Policy*, pp. 270, 273.

14. This legislation will be described in Chapter 3 of this book.

15. Jimmy Carter, *Keeping Faith: Memoirs of a President* (New York: Bantam Books, 1982), p. 143; and Jimmy Carter, *A Government As Good As Its People* (New York: Simon and Schuster, 1977), p. 71f.

16. Jimmy Carter, *Why Not the Best?* (New York: Bantam Books, 1976), p. 123.

17. Carter, *A Government As Good As Its People*, p. 166.

18. Ibid.

19. Carter, *Keeping Faith*, p. 143.

20. Ibid., p. 62.

21. Kucharsky, *The Man from Plains*, pp. 14, 43.

22. Bruce Mazlish and Edwin Diamond, *Jimmy Carter: A Character Portrait* (New York: Simon and Schuster, 1979), pp. 156, 158–160.

23. Ibid., p. 156, and Kucharsky, *The Man from Plains*, pp. 5, 115.

24. Kucharsky, *The Man from Plains*, pp. 13–14, 54, 68.

25. For social implications of the evangelical movement see Kucharsky, *The Man from Plains*, pp. 43, 77.

26. For Niebuhr's influence and quoted material see Mazlish and Diamond, *Jimmy Carter: A Character Portrait*, pp. 163–166.

27. Ibid., p. 167.

28. Kucharsky, *The Man from Plains*, p. 34.

29. Ibid., p. 41.

30. Carter, *Keeping Faith*, p. 142. The preceding discussion of Carter's background is based on Kucharsky, *The Man from Plains*, pp. 32–34, 41; Mazlish and Diamond, *Jimmy Carter: A Character Portrait*, pp. 203–205; and Carter, *Keeping Faith*, p. 142.

2

The Conceptual Framework for the Carter and Reagan Human Rights Policies

The first area of comparison between the human rights policies of the Carter and Reagan administrations is the conceptual framework within which each operated. "Conceptual framework" involves the following points, which will be the focus of this chapter:

1. Rationale: Why should human rights be an element in U.S. foreign policy?
2. Priorities: What place in foreign policy decision making is to be given to human rights?
3. Definition: What rights are to be promoted and protected?
4. Objectives: What purposes are to be served through the human rights policy?
5. Targets: Should the human rights policy be directed toward all human rights situations in other countries, or toward selected targets only?

RATIONALE

There are two general reasons why an administration would build human rights into its foreign policy: because this is the right thing to do, given this nation's moral values, or because doing so would serve American interests. Human rights, in other words, may be a foreign policy component as a matter of principle or of utility or of both.[1]

The Carter Administration

Statements by Jimmy Carter and key members of his administration strongly suggest that moral values were the main reason for a human rights emphasis in this administration. In his Inaugural Address, Carter declared, "Our commitment to human rights must be absolute. . . . Our moral sense dictates a clear-cut preference for those societies who share with us an abiding respect for individual human rights." Several months later, in a Notre Dame University commencement address, Carter reasserted that this country's commitment to human rights was "rooted in our moral values which never change,"[2] and that there should be a "new foreign policy based on common decency in its values."[3]

The moral tone of the Carter administration was reflected in the attitude of key personnel, as expressed, for example, by National Security Advisor Zbigniew Brzezinski: "We were determined to demonstrate also the primacy of the moral dimension of foreign policy."[4] Secretary of State Cyrus Vance saw the need for "harnessing our foreign policy to the basic values of our Founding Fathers" and "the championing of human rights" as "a requirement for a nation with our heritage."[5] And, finally, the foreign policy approach of Carter's assistant secretary of state for human rights and humanitarian affairs was well summed up in her statement that "you must also operate in a principled way."[6]

While the moral values tone was predominant in the rationale for the Carter administration's human rights foreign policy, the utilitarian or pragmatic element was by no means absent. Security Advisor Brzezinski, for example,

felt quite strongly that a major emphasis on human rights as a component of U.S. foreign policy would enhance America's global interests by demonstrating to the emerging nations of the Third World the reality of our democratic system, in sharp contrast to the political system and practices of our adversaries. The best way to answer the Soviets' ideological challenge would be to commit the United States to a concept which most reflected America's very essence.[7]

Evidence of pragmatism in the Carter administration's policy also came from Secretary of State Vance. In explaining how this administration was proceeding, he noted that "in each case [involving human rights considerations] we must balance a political concern for human rights against economic and security goals."[8]

The most authoritative spokesperson for the Carter administration's human rights policy, Patricia Derian, accepted pragmatic considerations as a legitimate reason for incorporating human rights in this country's foreign policy, but not as an alternative to or rival of moral values as a motivation.

Of course you must operate pragmatically, but you must also operate in a principled way, and I think that that's falling into a decision about whether it's going to be principled or whether it's going to be pragmatic as though there were some cleavage there, when there's no reason for there to be one at all.[9]

There were critics of the pragmatic element in the Carter human rights policy including historian Walter Laqueur. After noting that the Carter

administration had started with a "wonderful concept" and "the best intentions," Laqueur observed that "in the real world one has to make concessions
... but there has to be limits to concessions. I think there were too many
concessions."

In general, however, the Carter administration's human rights policy was
criticized not for its pragmatism but for what some observers saw as the lack
of realism. Ernest W. Lefever, for example, felt that Jimmy Carter suffered
from "a vague romantic optimism with an excessive confidence in the power
of reason and good will... underestimating the totalitarian threat and overestimating U.S. influence abroad, and ignoring the perils of reform intervention."[10]

Rather than seeing their human rights policy as prompted by either idealism or realism, Carter administration spokespersons preferred to justify it
on grounds that it combined the two. Thus Edmund S. Muskie, Cyrus
Vance's successor as secretary of state in Jimmy Carter's cabinet, declared,
"We do all this [promotion of human rights] not out of a naive idealism and
not only because it is right, [but]... we are also convinced, in the most
hard-headed and practical sense, that emphasis on human rights serves our
national interests."

In support of this thesis, Patricia Derian cited the cases of Greece, Soviet
oppression of Eastern Europe, Batista's Cuba, the shah's Iran, Park's Korea,
and Somosa's Nicaragua. These, in her opinion, were examples of the fact
that "we tried taking the line of least resistance on the human rights issue,"
and as a result of this "ignoring of human rights violations in the interests
of short-term expediency... we have paid a long-term price."[11]

The Reagan Administration

Like its predecessor, the Reagan administration saw human rights as de-
serving a place in U.S. foreign policy because inclusion of this issue was in
line with this country's values.

Human rights is at the core of American foreign policy because it is central to America's
conception of itself... Human rights is not something added to our foreign policy,
but its ultimate purpose: the preservation and promotion of liberty in the world....
This Administration believes that human rights is an issue of central importance...
to link foreign policy with the traditions of the American people.[12]

Statements like these, plus Secretary of State George Shultz's assertion that
"the President's philosophy is that... we find in our ideals a star to steer
by," suggest that moral values were included in the reasons for building
human rights into this country's foreign policy. Moral values as such, however, do not appear to be nearly so prominent in the rationale for the Reagan
human rights policy as the struggle against communism in general and the
U.S.-Soviet rivalry in particular.

Linking human rights in this way with the focus of the Reagan administration's foreign policy on opposing communism and the Soviet Union presents a real problem for anyone seeking to understand the rationale for the Reagan human rights policy, since it is not clear whether the motivation was principle or politics. One cannot be sure, in other words, whether communism and the Soviet Union were opposed because they were perceived to be antithetical to human rights, or whether the cause of human rights was supported because doing so was a good tactical weapon in the East-West struggle. The easy answer to this question, of course, is that there is room for both explanations. Opinions will obviously differ as to the validity of this answer, just as they will as to which of the alternatives really explains the Reagan policy.

While the Reagan administration's placing human rights within a geopolitical context is open to various interpretations, there can be no doubt that in this administration's eyes, "there is symmetry between promoting the geopolitical interests of the United States and promoting human rights,"[13] that to the Reagan administration "the Soviet Union is the overriding issue,"[14] and that to Reagan, "Communist countries are synonymous with human rights violations."[15] Thus, Elliott Abrams, while serving as assistant secretary of state for human rights and humanitarian affairs, included in one of his addresses the observation:

The conclusion we have to draw is that the East-West struggle matters a great deal for human rights. Let me acknowledge right now that I take the comment that this Administration puts human rights policy in an East-West framework to be descriptive rather than critical. To prevent any country from being taken over by a Communist regime is in our view a very real victory for the cause of human rights.[16]

The fact that the Reagan administration's policy was strongly anti-Communist, and that ideology was a major part of the administration's human rights policy has been noted by administrative personnel.[17] The same point was made in the Introduction to the State Department's *Country Reports on Human Rights Practices for 1981*:

It is a significant service to the cause of human rights to limit the influence the USSR [together with its clients and proxies] can exert. A consistent and serious policy for human rights in the world must counter the USSR politically and bring Soviet bloc human rights violations to the attention of the world over and over again.[18]

The ideological, geopolitical basis for the Reagan administration's human rights policy has drawn negative criticism from those who see it as a disservice to the cause of human rights and an approach that distorts policy. Thus one critic complains that this country's foreign policy has "been captured by a boarding party of ideologues. Everything is viewed through the Russian prism."[19] Another notes that "the human rights policy of this Administration is based on ideology, rather than law. Communism is seen as the worst human rights violation, and to prevent that, other abuses will be endured."[20] A third critical comment asserts that "to our Western European allies, U.S. policy seems anti-Soviet, not pro–human rights."[21]

PRIORITIES

The conceptual framework of the Carter and Reagan administrations' human rights policies is revealed not only in the official statements describing the rationale for a human rights policy, but in the kinds of decisions made when the pursuit of this policy appears to threaten the nation's security/ strategic interests. Decisions of this kind test and demonstrate an administration's priorities and provide insights into the place that the cause of human rights really holds in its thinking.

The question of the priority to be given to human rights is really a contemporary expression of the old debate between the "realists" and the "idealists" concerning which of these concepts should control policy. There has long been a tendency to assume that there is an inevitable conflict between a foreign policy concern for the physical security of the nation and the economic and social welfare of its citizens on one hand, and the belief that policy should reflect such national values as freedom and justice on the other.

If it is true that "there will always be a tension between our foreign policy as classically defined, in terms of U.S. economic, political, and security interests and our human rights interests," then choices must be made in specific situations.[22] If priority is given to national interest as narrowly and traditionally defined, the administration making this choice may be criticized for being hypocritical in proclaiming a commitment to American values but not putting this commitment into practice, for complicity in the human rights abuses of regimes that the United States supports for political/strategic reasons, or for wrong-headedness in sacrificing long-term American interests for the sake of the immediate benefits of association with politically friendly but oppressive regimes, regimes whose very nature raises questions concerning their stability.

If, on the other hand, an administration gives priority to human rights in a specific policy-making situation, it may be accused of being "utopian" in overestimating the ability of this country to effect changes in the conduct of other governments, who could be expected to resist intervention in their nation's internal affairs; of doing serious, immediate damage to American interests; or of creating situations in other countries that would prove to be worse, in respect to the observance of human rights, than those that were the targets of American action.

There could well be times, of course, when there would be no problem of priorities because considerations of national interest as traditionally defined and commitment to human rights clearly converge. In the absence of this convergence, however, an administration must make a choice between priorities, knowing that whatever decision it makes will be subject to criticism. An administration can, of course, seek to forestall or overcome such criticism. Thus, if the priority dilemma has been resolved in favor of human rights, the "realist" can be appeased by an assertion that a human rights policy is actually the most effective way to serve American interests in a given situation. If the resolution has given preference to political/security concerns, the administration can claim that this is really serving the cause of human rights, and thereby hope to satisfy the advocates of human rights. While the capacity of any administration to rationalize its policy decisions is beyond question, a similar ability to "sell" its explanations is not.

The response of the Carter and Reagan administrations to the need to set and follow priorities in policy decisions where the demands of human rights and political/security concerns were in conflict is the focus of this part of the analysis of the conceptual framework of these two administrations.

The Carter Administration

While holding a strong commitment to a human rights foreign policy the Carter administrations also expressed a determination to be flexible in dealing with specific situations. Therefore, dedication to the cause of human rights did not produce a rigid absolutism through which this issue would take precedence over all other foreign policy concerns in all cases. The Carter human rights policy, in short, was "far less single-minded than the Reagan Administration [for example] claims."[23] Typical of the Carter administration's approach was Secretary of State Cyrus Vance's assertion that "we had to be flexible and pragmatic in dealing with specific cases that might affect our national security and . . . had to avoid rigidity." He expressed this opinion in a lengthy discussion with President Carter, and there was no "significant disagreement" between them.[24]

Absolutism in regard to foreign policy priorities was thus rejected in favor of flexibility. The Carter administration proceeded on the assumption that a commitment to human rights did not demand an automatic priority for this factor in every decision but rather could be served by integrating it in an approach that took all concerns, including human rights, into consideration. President Carter and Secretary Vance shared a "commitment to weave the defense of human rights throughout the fabric of American foreign policy."[25] Noting that the problem of "how to integrate human rights into foreign policy has confronted every president since the Universal Declaration of Human Rights was adopted by the United Nations in 1948," one observer has commented that "no president has tried harder than Jimmy Carter" to achieve this incorporation.[26] That this effort at integration, rather than a doctrinaire approach, characterized the Carter administration is indicated by the remark of Michael Armacost of the State Department that "we have tried to recognize the need to integrate the security concerns of the United States with our human rights concerns."[27]

This emphasis on flexibility and integration expressed the Carter administration's intention that human rights should pass through a screening process at times of decision making. In this process all foreign policy concerns would be taken into account, with no presumption that any one factor would automatically dictate the decision. This assumption that a commitment to human rights did not mean that every foreign policy decision had to be made on that basis alone was accompanied by another: that this commitment could be fulfilled even when factors other than human rights were given a higher priority in the decision-making process. Carter's assistant secretary of state for human rights and humanitarian affairs, Patricia Derian, underscored this aspect of the policy:

Human rights remains a very high priority in foreign policy decision-making. There are also security interests which may require, on occasion, the provision of U.S. assistance to serious human rights violators. In such cases we have undertaken, in clear, direct, and persistent ways to emphasize our concerns about human rights conditions. [And for this purpose] the U.S. Government uses all other means at its disposal.[28]

Deputy Secretary of State Warren Christopher expressed the same belief:

I recognize that in many instances our security considerations will require us to continue programs of assistance to countries with poor human rights records, but one of the things I try to require of myself and of my associates is that we not fool ourselves when that happens. In other words, we should recognize openly that we are going ahead, despite poor human rights records. Moreover, we should make known our concerns about the human rights records in an appropriate way through diplomatic channels; we should explain that even though we are going to maintain this relationship for security reasons, we are concerned about what that country is doing from a human rights standpoint.[29]

The significance of this approach for the question of support for human rights becomes clearer when one considers the number of situations, real or alleged, where the Carter administration gave top priority to concerns other than human rights, including:

1. China, where "the decision to provide advanced technology was taken for purely strategic reasons. . . . Human rights factors were not weighed in that decision."[30]

2. South Korea, where "Carter was the latest of presidents to sacrifice human dignity on the altar of misperceived geopolitical factors or domestic political and economic considerations."[31] "As bad as its government's human rights policies are, we

certainly don't want the North Koreans to come in and take over. This would jeopardize regional security and our own, since we have a stake in the Pacific."[32]

3. East Timor/Indonesia, where "one of the most distressing aspects of the human rights situation was the role of the U.S. State Department . . . where the [Carter] Administration has accepted the annexation of East Timor by Indonesia, despite the violation [here] of the right of self-determination . . . out of a concern to protect the Suharto regime."[33]

4. The Philippines, where Filipino complaints about U.S. suppport for the Marcos dictatorship met with the response that "America is for freedom in the world; but above all we have our national security to protect. . . . And so President Carter was for human rights but gave Marcos a half-billion dollars."[34]

5. Panama, where "the administration's obstruction of information on human rights abuses persists, as does the policy of sustaining the dictatorship" and where Panama's human rights record is defended "in order to gain Congressional support for the Canal Treaty."[35]

Instances like these are not exceptions to a rule under which human rights consistently prevailed over all other considerations in the Carter administration's foreign policy making. On the contrary, a set of principles evidently guided the administration personnel responsible for policy decisions. One of the principles stated:

Human rights initiatives should be suspended or curtailed when they threaten other significant U.S. interests. Relations that are critical to U.S. well-being—Iran, the People's Republic of China, and Saudi Arabia, for example, should not be jeopardized by human rights initiatives. Moreover, short term efforts to bring about significant changes in bilateral relations should not be compromised by ill-timed human rights efforts.

The appearances of consistency further require that, when a country is exempted from human rights initiatives, other countries with which clear parallels can be made should also be exempted. Thus, North Korea and Vietnam are argued to be comparable to the People's Republic of China, and a number of Middle East countries to be comparable to Saudi Arabia.[36]

The extent to which this principle was followed led the author of one study of the Carter administration's human rights policy to conclude, "Military, economic, and strategic considerations were the final determinants in the formulation and application of foreign policy. Human rights became a subordinate factor when measured against the perceived imperatives of national security objectives."[37] The Carter administration's handling of the question of priorities, in other words, was such that, in Stephen Cohen's words, "the charge that its pursuit of human rights was 'single-minded' and to the exclusion of other interests was far wide of the mark."[38]

Whether or not this approach to policy priorities was characteristic of his administration throughout Carter's tenure in office or was a result of a change in his own foreign policy outlook in the later stages of his presidency is a debatable question. "In [his] final years Carter abandoned much of his earlier commitment to human rights . . . [so that] by the end of Carter's term it could well be asked if the administration had a human rights policy at all," assert Michael Klare and Cynthia Arnson. William Goodfellow concurs, alleging that Carter lost faith in the possibility of promoting both human rights and security interests.[39]

If there was, in fact, a change in the Carter administration's system of priorities as time went on, it could be traced to such events as the downfall of the shah of Iran and the Russian invasion of Afghanistan, and to the approaching presidential campaign, in which Carter was likely to be accused of having "lost" countries to factions unfriendly to the United States. A particularly sensitive area was the Caribbean, a region close to the United States and one alleged to be threatened by leftist influence from Cuba and Nicaragua. Here and in the broader area of Central and South America some saw a re-assertion of traditional U.S. security objectives and a consequent retreat from the human rights emphasis.[40]

The assertion that Carter's outlook on policy priorities changed over the years of his presidency, however, has been denied by some of the leading figures in his administration. National Security Advisor Bzrezinski, for example, has stated flatly, "Carter deeply believed in human rights and this commitment remained constant during his administration."[41] Carter's assistant secretary for human rights and humanitarian affairs, Patricia Derian, has denied that Carter "buckled" halfway through his term and lost interest in human rights, an opinion shared by one of her associates in this office, Mark Schneider, who has rejected as "not true" the contention that Carter lost faith in the possibility of serving both security interests and human rights. While "heavier weight" was given to the security side in Carter's later years, this was done "without discarding the view that, in the long run, security interests benefited from a human rights emphasis."[42]

While opinions differ as to whether the intensity of its concern for human rights diminished near the end of the Carter administration, it is clear that human rights did indeed enjoy a high priority during Carter's term in office. This conclusion stands despite the fact, noted previously, that this concern for human rights was not allowed to override security considerations.

Some critics even felt that the prominence of the human rights element in the Carter administration's foreign policy was carried too far. One such commentator, Lt. Gen. Gordon Sumner, Jr., contended that "U.S. security interests have been sacrificed on the altar of human rights without regard for the strategic consequences." Others accused the administration of "injecting a discordant note in U.S. policy deliberations" and "jeopardizing other U.S. foreign policy objectives."[43]

The human rights priority was evident in various actions, such as Carter's attempts to induce a better human rights performance on the part of the shah of Iran; similar efforts during a visit to South Korea; his supportive letter to Soviet dissident Andrey Sakharov, and his White House meeting with another Russian dissident, Vladimir Bukovsky. The Carter years also saw pro–human rights actions in South and Central America, including condemnation of Argentina for its violations of human rights and proposed reduction in military aid to this country because of these abuses, and strong criticism of Guatemala's regime, despite Guatemala's status as "the greatest prize . . . in terms of Central American geopolitics." This criticism led Guatemala to refuse further U.S. military aid. The administration also voted against international bank loans to countries with poor human rights records.[44] Deputy Secretary of State Warren Christopher saw another innovation in American diplomatic practice: "frank discussion of human rights in our consultations with foreign diplomats and leaders." "In the past," according to this official, "our diplomats tended to shy away from high-level dialogue on sensitive human rights issues such as the fate of political prisoners. Now those issues are raised in face-to-face conversation."[45]

The granting of a high priority to human rights was easier in some situations than in others, with the major variable being the presence or absence of the national security factor when policy decisions were being made. Thus it was apparently not too difficult to give precedence to human rights in decisions relating to the Western Hemisphere, where, as one study notes, there was a "relative absence of immediate threats to traditional security concerns."[46] In situations like this, where the security element was less prominent, the priority competition was with diplomatic and economic concerns. In such cases human rights enjoyed greater success in determining the direction policy was to take.[47]

The Reagan Administration

When Ronald Reagan took office in 1981, there was some indication that human rights would occupy a high place in the new administration's concerns. When asked whether the new administration would turn its back on human rights, one of its key spokespersons, Jeane Kirkpatrick, responded "absolutely not."[48] Secretary of State Alexander M. Haig, Jr., gave a "resounding 'yes' " to the question of whether a concern for human rights was compatible with the pursuit of this country's interests. Secretary Haig also expressed his anticipation that "every regional policy director will have human rights high on his agenda in his across-the-board assessment of what is in the vital interests of this country." While he stated that terrorism would replace human rights in the administration's concerns, he qualified this shift by explaining that terrorism is "the ultimate abuse of human rights," a comment that could be interpreted as an endorsement of human rights as the end to be served.[49] Finally, the Reagan administration's first edition of the *Country*

Reports on Human Rights Practices included the assertion that "this administration believes that human rights is an issue of central importance."[50]

Counterbalancing these professions of concern for human rights are indications that the incoming administration would assign a much lower priority to this issue than did the Carter administration. National Security Advisor Richard Allen, for example, stated that the new administration "would not place as much ideological emphasis on human rights" as did its predecessor, and the report submitted by Reagan's transition planning team included the recommendation that "internal policy-making procedures should be structured to ensure that human rights is not in a position to paralyze or unduly delay decisions on which human rights concerns conflict with the vital United States interests."[51]

Actions taken by the new administration suggest that this recommendation was accepted and that it did, in fact, assign a lower priority to human rights than this concern had previously enjoyed. These actions included the reversal of Carter administration policies, motivated by a human rights concern, vis-à-vis a number of states with poor human rights records, such as:

1. Chile, whose refusal to extradite persons suspected of assassinating a Chilean exile leader in Washington led to Carter-imposed trade sanctions, which the Reagan administration then relaxed.

2. South Korea, whose president, head of a military government with a record of rights abuses, was accorded the honor of being the first foreign head of state to visit the White House after Ronald Reagan took office. Reagan praised Chun Doo Hwan as a "man of freedom."

3. El Salvador, where 9,000 persons were killed in political violence the previous year, and where the United States had been insisting on a government investigation into the murder of four American churchwomen as a condition for the granting of U.S. economic and military aid. The Reagan administration dropped this insistence.

4. Argentina, whose military regime had been condemned by the Inter-American Human Rights Commission, and for whom military aid had been suspended by the Carter administration on human rights grounds; and

5. Brazil, where, like Argentina, such human rights abuses as political killings and torture had brought public condemnation and the dropping of military aid under Reagan's predecessor. In both cases, the Reagan administration's change in priorities from human rights to hemispheric security was expressed in the extension of invitations to military leaders from these countries to come to Washington for talks.[52]

Other actions taken in the early stages of the Reagan administration provide additional evidence that one characteristic of this administration at that time was a low priority for human rights. These actions included support in international financial institutions for loans to countries with poor human rights records and the appointment of certain assistant secretaries of state to head regional bureaus, which was seen as "insuring a loss for human rights."[53] Nomination of Ernest W. Lefever as assistant secretary of state for human rights and humanitarian affairs was seen as a "clear signal of the Reagan Administration's contempt for human rights"[54] because his sincerity in the area of human rights was suspect. He believed, for example, that "the United States should remove from the statute books all clauses that establish a human rights standard or condition that must be met by another government before our government transacts normal business with it."[55]

When the opposition to the Lefever nomination proved to be strong enough to defeat it, this was seen as a "defeat for the reaction to the Carter human rights emphasis."[56] Having been rebuffed in his attempt to place Ernest Lefever at the head of the Human Rights Bureau, Reagan allowed nearly a year to go by before submitting another nominee for this post, which did little to enhance his image as a president with a real concern for human rights. During this period of presidential inaction administration and State Department personnel were engaged in a lively debate. Some urged a re-thinking of the administration's original attitude toward human rights. This debate culminated in a memorandum to Secretary Haig recommending a basic change in policy toward a more positive acceptance of human rights.

Secretary Haig approved the memorandum, which stated, "Human rights is at the core of our foreign policy because it is central to what America stands for" and described "overall foreign policy" as being "based on a strong human rights policy." Shortly after the submission of this document, Elliott Abrams, the memorandum's author, was nominated to the vacant human rights post and was subsequently approved. The White House ac-companied the nomination with a statement reiterating the place of human rights in the administration's foreign policy. Said President Reagan, "The promotion of liberty has always been a central element of our nation's foreign policy. In my administration, human rights considerations are important in all aspects of our foreign policy."

Other administration personnel, reacting to the storm of protest brought on by the Lefever nomination, also issued statements asserting that human rights did indeed occupy a prominent place in the administration's policy making. Thus Secretary Haig, speaking shortly after the Lefever rejection, stated, "Human rights are not only compatible with our national interests [but] are the major focus of our foregn policy." Two months later UN Ambassador Jeane Kirkpatrick declared that the idea that the Reagan admin-istration was not concerned with human rights was a "myth."[57]

Late 1981 marked the end of the first phase of the Reagan administration's treatment of human rights as a foreign policy component and the beginning of the second, in which there was some evidence that human rights enjoyed a higher status. Several factors produced this change. One was the resistance to the Lefever nomination, demonstrating that human rights had strong support both among the general public and in the Congress. Another was the administration's growing awareness as a result of the experience of some months in office of the policy and procedural demands of human rights laws, demands that had to be satisfied regardless of any administration's own attitude. A third factor was the outcome of the debate within the bureaucracy following the Lefever episode over the place of human rights, leading to Elliott Abrams's memorandum. Finally, there was the existence of the Bureau of Human Rights and Humanitarian Afairs, an agency mandated by a Congress that could be counted on to see that it was given the personnel and other resources to function effectively.[58]

The net effect of these and perhaps other influences was that events in the next few years seemed to indicate that human rights enjoyed a higher status in the Reagan administration's system of priorities. Thus, in 1983 both U.S. Ambassador Thomas Pickering and Vice-President George Bush publicly denounced the death squad killings and disappearances in El Salvadore. The vice-president's denunciation was accompanied by a warning that U.S. aid to this country would cease if its government did not end these human rights violations. The situation in Haiti also drew criticism from the Reagan administration, which Ambassador Clayton McManaway expressed directly to President Jean-Claude Duvalier. The ambassador emphasized his government's concern for the status of human rights in Haiti by inviting opposition political leaders, many of whom had been targets of Duvalier's oppressive policies, to an embassy reception.[59]

A third country in which human rights violations drew a critical response from the Reagan administration was the Philippines, whose president, Ferdinand Marcos, had compiled a dismal record in this regard. Despite this record, U.S. Vice-President George Bush in 1981 had lauded Marcos's "adherence to democratic principles and the democratic process," and the dictator had been described by President Reagan in 1982 as "a respected voice for reason and moderation." The 1983 murder of opposition leader Benigno Aquino, however, marked the beginning of a change in the Reagan position vis-à-vis Marcos. The first indication of this change was the cancellation by the United States of Reagan's proposed visit to the Philippines in November, an action generally seen as a move away from Marcos.[60] The process of distancing the U.S. from Filipino President Marcos continued in 1984 and subsequent years, reaching a climax in the positive role played by the Reagan administration in Marcos's downfall in 1986.

The Reagan administration also cited a number of Communist countries for human rights violations—not surprising, given the strong anti-Communist orientation of this administration. Cuba, for example, was subjected to severe criticism, and the United States used its influence on behalf of persecuted Hungarian intellectuals. Human rights violations in the Soviet Union were the topic of strong public statements by Reagan and senior administration officials, and State Department releases called attention to arrests and trials of Russian human rights activists. And, finally, the United States engaged in a joint Roundtable with Romania in February 1984, in the course of which the question of human rights in Romania was "forcefully" raised by the American delegation head, Elliott Abrams.[61]

Additional evidence that the Reagan administration was giving a high priority to human rights lies in the procedures for decisions about assistance to other countries. Thus Assistant Secretary of State Elliott Abrams testified:

The Interagency Working Group on Human Rights and Foreign Assistance . . . considers human rights practices in every country for which bilateral aid and/or multilateral development loans are being planned. . . . Human rights considerations are a key factor in examining and determining military assitance levels and where security and economic considerations are integral to the process.[62]

To these examples of a more positive approach to the question of human rights after the Reagan Administration's first months in office can be added Reagan's International Human Rights Day statement at the White House ceremony on December 10, 1985, which was seen as "demonstrating how far the administration has come in committing itself to promoting human rights internationally." Progress was also seen in the fact that an annual celebration of Human Rights Day had become a Reagan White House institution.[63]

Thus, there is evidence that after its first year in office, the Reagan administration began to give a more prominent place to human rights in its foreign policy concerns. Nevertheless, some negative aspects of Reagan's record renewed the question of how high a place this issue actually held in the administration's system of priorities.

Latin America is one area where the Reagan administration's performance raised doubts concerning the degree of its concern for human rights. In El Salvador, for example, the administration's role was seen as that of "an apologist for some of the worst horrors of our time." Some of these horrors were denounced by the American embassy, and the State Department's report on the situation in El Salvador called attention to such rights abuses as violations of freedom of speech and association, torture, and killings. This record of abuses, however, did not prevent the Reagan administration from continuing military aid to El Salvador, justifying this policy with the argument that the human rights situation in this country was "improving."[64]

Guatemala is another Latin American country where the Reagan administration's response to an unsavory record raised doubts as to its commitment to human rights. Thus, despite the killings attributed to its leader, Rios Montt, Reagan declared that the Guatemalan government was the victim of a "bum rap" and expressed the opinion that Guatemala deserved renewed military aid.[65]

The Reagan administration's dealings with other Latin American situations produced additional indications of a low-level concern for human rights. One study of its Latin American policy concluded that the administration "failed to concern itself in any visible way with human rights" in either Peru or Colombia and noted that American ambassadors to Uruguay and Chile "distanced themselves from human rights victims and human rights monitors, [conveying] the impression that the United States [did] not care about human rights."[66]

In other areas of the world the Reagan administration's human rights record also invited negative criticism. Turkey, for example, was the scene of serious human rights abuses; but probably motivated by geopolitical considerations, the Reagan administration defended this country's record and, according to one study, "disparaged Turkey's critics."[67] Again, U.S. aid continued to go to Zaire, despite its record of human rights violations and even though human rights concerns were said to be "central to our policy toward Zaire." Assistant Secretary of State Abrams, who made this assertion, explained the apparent anomaly by adding that human rights are "only one aspect of a complex and critical bilateral relationship."[68]

Another situation where the Reagan administration's performance cast doubts as to its concern for human rights was Pakistan, which continued to receive military aid despite the "very grim" human rights conditions there. Pakistan was pictured as "a champion of freedom in a troubled area": here as elsewhere, in the Reagan lexicon, "freedom" actually meaning "anticommunism." Reagan justified continued support for Pakistan on the grounds that this assistance was going to the country as such, not to Pakistan's President Zia ul-Haq, whose regime was responsible for the abuses of human rights in this country.

Reagan administration officials also defended the U.S. policy toward Pakistan by asserting that the Asian subcontinent was too complicated an area for the United States to understand, that when a "competent ruler such as Pakistan's Zia" defines a situation in a certain way, the U.S. government is not qualified to dispute this definition.[69] A critical observer could easily see a protective disclaimer like this as an additional reason to doubt the intensity of the administration's commitment to human rights. The administration did not hesitate to condemn human rights violations in other situations that to an unbiased observer would seem to be at least as complicated as that in Pakistan. The defense of the administration's position vis-à-vis Pakistan, in other words, is so weak as to lead to the conclusion that the only motivating factor here was a preference for security over its rival concern, human rights. A frank statement to this effect would be preferable to an unconvincing assertion that the administration was facing a situation "too complicated" to permit an American assessment.

DEFINITION OF HUMAN RIGHTS

A third element in the conceptual framework within which each administration formed and implemented its human rights policy is the definition of the term itself. What did "human rights" mean to the Carter administration, and what did it mean to the Reagan administration?

In defining human rights, the approach most generally taken is to identify two broad categories of such rights: civil/political and economic/social. This approach was given formal recognition by the United Nations in producing two instruments: the Covenant on Economic, Social, and Cultural Rights and the Covenant on Civil and Political Rights. While there are thus two categories of human rights, they have been aptly described as being "interdependent" and "of comparable value."[70] This viewpoint was expressed in 1975 by the U.S. ambassador to the UN, John Scali:

Let us therefore stop quibbling whether the right to a fair trial is more or less important than the right to have one's children fed adequately. I can agree with those who argue that political freedom means little to the human being who lacks food to eat. I would insist, however, that hunger for freedom and hunger for bread go hand in hand. Economic democracy means little without political democracy.[71]

The two categories of human rights are not always accorded equal status, however, as the following discussion will demonstrate.

The Carter Administration

The Carter administration defined human rights as those that the UN General Assembly proclaimed in the Universal Declaration of Human Rights adopted in 1946, and hence Carter went beyond the civil/political rights focus of the human rights legislation enacted by the U.S. Congress.[72] Secretary of State Cyrus Vance in his Law Day Address at the University of Georgia, on April 30, 1977, clearly expressed this inclusiveness by giving this elaboration of the traditional two-category definition:

1. The right to be free from governmental violation of the integrity of the person: torture; cruel, inhuman or degrading treatment or punishment; arbitrary arrest or imprisonment; denial of a fair, public trial; invasion of the home.

2. The right to the fulfillment of such vital needs as food, shelter, health care, and education.

3. The right to enjoy civil and political liberties: freedom of thought, religion, assembly, speech, press, movement both within and outside one's own country, and freedom to take part in government.

The Carter administration thus distinctly included economic and social rights in its concept of what rights are to be promoted and protected, and identified the integrity of the person, generally subsumed under civil/political rights, as a separate category. This three-fold definition of human rights provided the framework for the State Department's *Country Reports on Human Rights*

Practices, which described each country's degree of adherence to each of the three categories. The equal standing accorded all these groups of rights was emphasized by Assistant Secretary of State Warren Christopher who said, "We attach fundamental importance to all three categories of internationally recognized human rights."[73] The administration's attitude toward the three sets of rights was given additional expression in the comment by Patricia Derian of the Human Rights Bureau that "the human rights policy of the United States has always strongly emphasized the inter-relationship of these rights."[74]

The Reagan Administration

The most distinctive feature of the Reagan administration's definition of human rights was the refusal to consider economic/social norms as "rights." Philosophically opposed to the idea of economic/social rights as such, the administration preferred to consider the economic/social elements in the Universal Declaration of Human Rights to be "hortatory," that is, as goals or objectives toward which national societies should strive, but not as rights.

The Reagan administration made its position clear on the question of what it meant by human rights in its first edition of *Country Reports on Human Rights Practices*. The "internationally recognized human rights" were divided into two categories: (1) the right to be free from such violations of the integrity of the person as torture, and (2) the right to enjoy such civil and political liberties as freedom of speech. The introduction to the reports for 1981 also explained the administration's elimination of economic/social rights in its catalog of those to be protected. It asserted:

the idea of economic and social rights is easily abused by repressive governments which claim that they promote human rights even though they deny their citizens the basic rights to the integrity of the person, as well as civil and political rights. This justification for repression has in fact been extensively used. No category of rights should be allowed to become an excuse for the denial of other rights. For this reason, the term economic and social rights is, for the most part, not used in this year's reports.[75]

The Reagan administration dropped economic/social rights for other reasons as well. It believed that if civil/political rights are respected, economic/social rights "can take care of themselves." The administration also contended that while governments could be expected to implement such civil/political rights as freedom from torture, participation in government, and fair trials they could not give the same immediate, clear effect to the considerations generally included in economic/social rights, such as full employment and health care. The implementation of these rights, it was further argued, could not be achieved without a degree of control that would open the door to repression. Obviously, such extensive controls are unacceptable to the Reagan administration, given its conviction that primary responsibility for economic/social matters rests with the private sector.[76]

The Reagan administration's rejection of economic/social rights as rights places it in opposition not only to the Carter administration's definition of human rights, but to the definition that has been established in international law, whose primary source is treaties. In such treaties as the United Nations International Covenant on Economic, Social, and Cultural Rights and the Social Charter of the Council of Europe we find clear evidence that international law regards economic/social rights as rights.

The existence of the Social Charter, which has been in effect since 1965 and whose parties include the major democracies of Western Europe, calls into serious question one of the Reagan administration's reasons for rejecting economic/social rights as rights: their alleged relationship to repression. The fact that civil/political rights are very much alive and quite healthy in the democracies of Western Europe demonstrates the obvious: that there is no inherent, necessary link between economic/social rights and repression.

Again the claim that economic/social rights take longer to implement than civil/political rights seems to argue that (1) the validity of a set of rights depends on their capability for implementation, and (2) the process by which effect is given to rights, and the immediacy with which this effect can be achieved, must be the same for all kinds of rights. The vulnerability of a claim like this to debate and refutation is obvious.

Equally obvious is the Reagan administration's determination to hold to its view that economic/social rights do not belong in a definition of human rights. Thus, even though the administration complied with the provisions of Title V of the Trade and Tariff Act of 1984 by including information on workers' rights in the *Country Reports on Human Rights Practices for 1985*, it did so without altering the pattern of categories of rights followed in the reports. Some of the workers' rights identified in the new legislation were dealt with under the heading of civil rights, while the remainder were treated in the section describing the economic, social, and cultural situation prevailing in each country.[77]

HUMAN RIGHTS POLICY OBJECTIVES

The Carter Administration

The Carter administration's human rights policies apparently had a number of objectives, one of which was humanitarian: to improve the human condition in other countries or as the head of Carter's Human Rights Bureau put it, "do what we can to improve the condition of human rights around the world." This broad humanitarian objective carried with it certain corollary or supportive purposes: to win freedom and/or better conditions for political prisoners and other victims of oppression, reduce worldwide government violations of the integrity of the person, enhance political and civil liberties, and promote basic economic and social rights. Along the same lines, the policy was designed to provide encouragement and support for human rights activists in other countries and, in Carter's words, "to support the efforts of other nations to build their own institutions in ways that will meet the irrepressible human drive for freedom and justice." Multilateral and bilateral initiatives were to be undertaken, as Carter's national security advisor Zbigniew Brzezinski noted, to "influence other governments to give a higher priority to human rights." President Carter and others further defined the objectives of the administration's human rights policy to be not the imposition of American institutions and systems on others, but the "enhancing of respect, worldwide, for internationally recognized human rights."

The Carter administration's objectives included political and security concerns. Thus, according to Brzezinski, "we wanted to match Soviet ideological expansion by a more affirmative American posture on global human rights." It was hoped, too, that this posture would also serve America's security interests by helping increase the number of rights-respecting governments, since these countries would presumably be forces for international peace and stability. Furthermore, there was a feeling that this country's strategic interests would be well served by the projection of an image of the United States as both powerful and human.

Finally, the Carter administration sought to disassociate this country from governments that were guilty of serious human rights violations. Speaking to this point, Patricia Derian asserted that the United States "should not give official sanction to the repression of human beings by other governments ... through ... U.S. aid.... And so part of [the policy] is to distance ourselves."[78]

The Reagan Administration

As *Country Reports on Human Rights Practices for 1982* stated, one of the objectives of the human rights policy of the Reagan administration was the humanitarian goal of "seeking to improve human rights practices in numerous countries—to eliminate torture or brutality[and] to secure religious freedom." One aspect of the humanitarian purpose underlying the administration's human rights policy was a strong emphasis on the promotion of democratic institutions and practices in other countries, a goal that President Reagan described as "the fostering of the infrastructure of democracy." He denied that this objective constituted cultural imperialism. If the goal of the democratization of these societies could be reached, it was argued, then the broader humanitarian purposes would be much more easily attained; "the rights of individuals are most effectively promoted and expanded by and through democratic political institutions."

The objectives of the Reagan administration's human rights policy also had their political/security component. Thus, a concern for human rights was seen as compatible with this country's national interests because, in the words of Secretary of State Alexander Haig, "We want a world hospitable to our society and our common ideals." The evidence of a strong concern for human rights, moreover, was felt to be important to sustaining good relations with this country's "most stable, reliable allies, who are democracies." Again, the clear association of the United States with the cause of liberty was seen as a way "to win international cooperation and defeat anti-American propaganda."

Human Rights Bureau head Elliott Abrams identified a third objective of the Reagan administration's human rights policy in testimony to a congressional subcommittee: the administration had "a commitment to utilize U.S. assistance programs . . . to distance the United States from violations of human rights." This objective, however, was not permitted to interfere with the pursuit of another purpose which the administration saw as a human rights objective: resistance to communism, a policy goal to which the administration gave the highest priority. The relationship between the objective of distancing the United States from rights abusers, on one hand, and that of resisting the expansion of communism, on the other, was clearly stated by Abrams: "The United States is at times reluctantly compelled to support regimes which abuse human rights because we think their replacements [leftist systems] would be much worse for the cause of human rights."[79]

HUMAN RIGHTS POLICY TARGETS

The final point in this discussion of the conceptual framework within which the human rights policies of the Carter and Reagan administrations were formed and implemented concerns the targets of these policies: the national situations toward which human rights initiatives were directed. The question is whether the administrations followed the principle of evenhandedness, holding all governments to the same standards and responding with equal intensity to all situations where rights were being violated, or whether they proceeded selectively, applying different standards from country to country and dealing with some situations more vigorously than others. In other words, did these administrations feel that their commitment to the protection of human rights should be applied consistently and uniformly across the global board?

The case for consistency or evenhandedness in the selection of targets includes:

1. If expressions of concern for human rights abuses are to be effective, they must be directed to all such instances. A government to whom the United States makes representations concerning human rights is far less likely to take these initiatives

seriously if it has reason to feel that it has been singled out for special treatment for political reasons. The United States must therefore respond with equal promptness and intensity to all situations of rights abuses if it is to lessen the opportunity for a target government to evade the human rights issue by accusing the United States of using human rights as a political instrument.

2. If it is true that maintaining the moral integrity of this country requires the inclusion of human rights in U.S. foreign policy, then this country must act in response to all situations of rights abuses. Actions must be taken in defense of human rights simply because the United States is the kind of nation that it is; the identity of the country where rights are being violated is irrelevant. The moral integrity of the United States can be preserved only by disassociating this country from all regimes guilty of abusing the rights of their people.

3. If the purpose of a human rights policy is truly that of helping people in other countries to live a better life, then people everywhere deserve to be included in U.S. efforts in defense of human rights, and these efforts should be just as vigorous in one situation as another. No people should be deprived of whatever good these efforts might accomplish simply because they live in certain countries.

There is also a case to be made for the principle of selectivity in the matter of targets for a human rights policy for the following reasons:

1. The human rights policy of an American administration should bear most heavily on abusive governments that are political friends of the United States because (1) the chances of gaining improvements in the human rights situations of these countries are greater than they are in respect to some other nations, since the United States presumably has more influence or leverage with them than with regimes that are less friendly or openly hostile to the United States; (2) such actions are necessary if the United States is not to be charged with complicity in the abuses of human rights committed by regimes to whose advent to and/or continuation in power the United States has been a substantial contributor.[80]

2. As a converse to point 1 political considerations require that the United States treat the human rights situations in friendly countries with special leniency in order to avoid the risk of destabilizing their regimes and thus creating an opportunity for less friendly factions to come to power.

3. Politically unfriendly governments should be targeted for particularly vigorous application of U.S. human rights policy, because such actions could weaken the position of these governments both at home and in the world community.

4. Governments that are held to pose the greatest threats to human rights should be singled out for particularly strenuous efforts to apply U.S. human rights policy; for some, this means special attention to Communist/leftist regimes.

The problem of choosing between evenhandedness and selectivity in identifying the targets for actions in defense of human rights is complicated by several factors that must be considered in any discussion of the policies of the Carter and Reagan administrations. One is the availability of information.

Thus, an administration may fail to make a strong response to a particular situation simply because it lacks information, not because it prefers selectivity as a guiding principle. Again, the choice of targets may be based on a preference for relativism rather than absolutism in the application of a human rights policy. The question, in other words, is whether the human rights performance of all governments should be judged by the same standards, or whether cultural, historical, and other factors should be taken into account in determining what can or should be expected of governments in particular national situations.

"Evenhandedness" thus becomes much more than a simplistic adoption of the same measures to deal with all human rights situations throughout the world. Some governments may be targeted for particularly intensive human rights efforts because a higher level of human rights performance can reasonably be expected of them. In such cases the administration that follows this policy may actually be evenhanded in its approach, in that it is dealing with all countries in terms of their actual capacity for certain levels of performance.

In assessing administrations on the basis of how they approach the question of selection of targets, it is also important to remember that this aspect of human rights policy is highly susceptible to the impact of events and circumstances. Thus, an administration's apparently particularly close attention to some human rights situations to the neglect of others may or may not reflect a decision to base the choice of targets on the principle of selectivity. Rather, such unevenness may merely follow from such prosaic but significant factors as the time available to personnel to deal with all instances that could be on the human rights agenda, or the level of intensity of conflict among advocates of the various interests competing for a policy priority and the outcome of this struggle, or the intensity of the pressure from Congress.

The Carter Administration

According to some of its critics, the Carter administration operated on the basis of selectivity rather than evenhandedness in the application of its human rights policy, and certain actions taken by this administration support this thesis. These citations, however, involve types of targets that contrast in nature so greatly as to create doubts as to their usefulness as evidence of selectivity. Thus, as the following examples will demonstrate, some critics accused the Carter administration of putting too much stress on human rights violations in rightist countries friendly to the United States, to the relative neglect of bad situations in Communist states, while others took just the opposite view, charging the administration with unduly emphasizing the abuses in hostile, mainly Communist, nations.

The feeling apparently existed within the Carter administration itself that the human rights policy was directed too much against rightist governments to whom the United States looked for political support. Thus National Security Advisor Brzezinski notes that he was "concerned that our human rights policy was in danger of becoming too one-sidedly anti-rightist" and feared that the United States was "running the risk of having bad relations simultaneously with Brazil, Chile, and Argentina" because of the way the human rights policy was being implemented.

Expressions of a similar viewpoint came from outside the administration, as for example the testimony by Lt. Gen. Gordon Sumner, Jr. (Ret.) to a congressional subcommittee that "our traditional friends under this [human rights] policy have been pilloried while the human rights transgressions of Fidel Castro are overlooked." By "traditional friends" he meant Latin American nations that he felt were being made victims of a new form of U.S. interventionism through the Carter human rights policy. Ernest W. Lefever also charged that the administration's human rights policy was biased against friendly states in his assertion that Carter administration personnel and the State Department "frankly admit that they give more critical attention to allies than to adversaries because they have more leverage over the former."

Other critics of the Carter administration's human rights policy took just the opposite view of which countries were the victims of the administration's alleged lack of evenhandedness. According to these observers, the Communist states were the special targets of the Carter policy. "More often than not," opined one, "Carter spoke out more vigorously against human rights abuses in the Soviet Union and Eastern Europe than against those Third World dictatorships where the United States had historically contributed to repression, thus using human rights to promote a new Cold War." Again, critical attention was called to the refusal by the United States to grant most-favored-nation trade status to the Soviet Union on human rights grounds. This position stood in direct contrast to the treatment accorded to China and Taiwan in this respect, even though these two were also guilty of rights violations. The difference, according to this source, was that China and Taiwan were classed as present or potential political friends of the United States, while the Soviet Union was viewed as an adversary. Some observers saw such actions as further evidence of what they perceived to be the administration's tendency "to apply the human rights policy selectively to those countries with which the United States was in political tension." This tension, of course, was most severe in relations between the United States and certain Communist states, notably the Soviet Union and Cuba.

There is also a third category of states singled out for special treatment under the Carter administration's human rights policy: countries that were of strategic importance to the United States. This possibility is suggested, for example, by Stephen B. Cohen's discussion of the Carter administration's application of the "extraordinary circumstances" basis for extending U.S. aid to governments with poor human rights records. This justification was used concerning Indonesia because this country was held to be a counterweight to Soviet and Vietnamese influence in Southeast Asia; Iran because of its long border with the Soviet Union, its oil supply, and its willingness to contribute to the defense of American interests in the Persian Gulf; South Korea because of its service as a deterrent to North Korean expansion; the Philippines because of the American military bases located there; and Zaire because it was the source of most of the cobalt needed by aircraft producers in the West.[81]

While some critics of the Carter administration saw selectivity at work in the implementation of its human rights policy, others found reason to believe that the administration was trying to be evenhanded in its approach. One observer credited this administration with "having made it clear that it wanted to go beyond the identification of a limited number of egregious violators and use its influence . . . to improve human rights conditions in a wide range of countries." Congressman Donald Fraser, a vigorous promoter of human rights, testified that he "didn't see a problem of lack of even-handedness on the part of the administration." And in a comment that was really intended to reflect negatively on Carter's human rights policy, Jeane Kirkpatrick stated, "Carter measured all countries by the same standards."

Patricia Derian, head of the Human Rights Bureau, substantiated Carter's commitment to evenhandedness, saying that "in evaluating the human rights performance [of Asian Communist countries] we apply the same standards as we do to all other countries; . . . we make policy evenhandedly and objectively." Deputy Secretary of State Warren Christopher agreed that "we have raised human rights issues on a regular basis with every country with which we maintain diplomatic relations." Derian further observed that, at the 1980 session of the UN's Commission on Human Rights, "the United States strongly supported efforts to insure that the United Nations acts evenhandedly in applying human rights criteria to all countries."[82]

Perhaps the strongest argument for the thesis that the Carter administration was committed to an evenhanded approach to the implementation of its human rights policy is the conflicting claims by those who contend that the administration was intent on singling out certain countries for special attention. When some critics accuse an administration of singling out Communist regimes as special targets for human rights action while others allege that it is particularly hard on right-wing regimes, it is fair to assume that the administration in question comes as close to being evenhanded as possible, faced as it is with all the factors that complicate the implementation of any aspect of foreign policy.

The Reagan Administration

The Reagan administration assumed office in 1981 with the announced intention of dealing in an evenhanded manner with violations of human rights in other countries. "The new administration," said State Department spokesman William Dyess, "is determined to focus attention on all human rights abuses wherever they occur," and this commitment to evenhandedness was renewed in the administration's first issue of *Country Reports on Human Rights Practices* in 1981, which asserted, "U.S. human rights policy will not pursue a policy of selective indignation."

Other spokesmen for the administration repeated this official dedication to the principle of evenhandedness in subsequent years. In 1983 Human Rights Bureau head Elliott Abrams assured a congressional subcommittee that in the preparation of the *Country Reports* "we attempt to avoid allowing politics to determine the portraits they contain." The following year an address by Secretary of State Shultz included the comment that:

if we were never seriously concerned about human rights abuses in friendly countries, our policy would be one-sided and cynical. Thus, while the Soviet Union and its proxies present the most profound and farreaching danger to human rights, we cannot let it appear—falsely—that this is our only human rights concern. It is not.[83]

In the same year the introduction to the *Country Reports on Human Rights Practices for 1984* said:

In line with the theme set early in the Reagan Administration, the United States has continued to insist in international forums on a policy of evenhandedness in dealing with human rights violations throughout the world.

The difference between what the Reagan administration professed and the perception on this point is well expressed in an International Commission of Jurists publication:

Described as a "blunt, articulate defender of a policy that tends to excoriate left-wing and Communist regimes and mutes criticisms of such rightist countries as the Philippines, South Korea, Taiwan, and South Africa", Abrams insists that the Reagan Administration seeks evenhandedly to mitigate human rights violations wherever necessary and regardless of the political complexion of the government in question.[84]

While the Reagan administration may have been officially committed to the principle of evenhandedness in its response to human rights situations, its actions led many observers to conclude that it had really chosen to operate selectively. Thus one review of the administration's performance in its first two years in office found that this administration "had cheapened the currency of human rights by invoking its principles to criticize governments it perceives to be hostile to the United States and by denying or justifying abuses by governments it perceives as friendly to the United States." In another review, the administration was charged with failure to practice evenhandedness in the proceedings of the UN's Commission on Human Rights in two sessions in the early 1980s. In these sessions, according to a spokesman for a human rights group, the United States employed a double standard by voting to condemn Poland but not Guatemala and by "inveighing against the Soviet Union, Cuba, and Nicaragua" while failing to condemn El Salvador.[85]

Criticisms of the Reagan administration for implementing its human rights policy selectively continued to appear. In a 1984 hearing on the question of torture, one witness expressed the opinion:

One reason the administration has been less effective than it should be in organizing condemnation of torture in countries such as Iran and Afghanistan is that the United States is not perceived worldwide as . . . an evenhanded country condemning torture wherever it is practiced.[86]

Evidence that the president and his administration had failed to shed their "selective" image appeared in a *New York Times* editorial in October 1985, which criticized the president for "castigating" the Soviet Union at a Geneva summit meeting but failing to say anything about apartheid in South Africa or "the lack of political liberty" in South Korea, Chile, and the Philippines. In August the same paper had protested the administration's practice of denouncing the "totalitarian dungeon" close to the southern border of the United States [Nicaragua] while "rarely speaking out" concerning a country which "best fits his description: Haiti."[87] Selectivity was also seen in the administration's handling of the refugee problem. Thus, in the words of one commentator,

People who are leaving Communist countries are presumed to be political refugees, while people fleeing from non-Communist countries, no matter how much they say they fear persecution, are economic refugees. Thus the administration decided that Nicaraguans who request asylum will be treated as political refugees while refugees from El Salvador are automatically sent back—no matter how much they claim they are fleeing persecution.[88]

The point, of course, is that granting political asylum to certain refugees is in a sense an acknowledgment that a particular government is oppressive, to the point where people feel compelled to seek refuge elsewhere. This, it is alleged, is a concession that the Reagan administration was not willing to make concerning politically friendly regimes, such as El Salvador. There was obviously no such reluctance in regard to Communist regimes.

The Reagan administration's selectivity in implementing its human rights policy was an almost inevitable consequence of the rationale on which its foreign policy was based. This rationale, which posited Soviet/Communist expansionism as the principal threat to U.S. interests, pervaded and guided all aspects of the administration's foreign policy, including human rights. When the administration's anticommunism thrust entered the area of human rights, it carried with it a division of nondemocratic political systems into two categories: authoritarian and totalitarian, dictatorships of the right and left, respectively. While human rights violations could be found in both of these nondemocratic systems, the Reagan philosophy maintained that the two differed in two significant respects: (1) authoritarian regimes were said to be redeemable, capable of evolving into rights-respecting democracies, but the same could not be said concerning totalitarian systems; and (2) authoritarian regimes, in the main, were politically friendly to the United States, but those of a totalitarian nature tended to be either unfriendly or hostile to this country.

The implementation of the Reagan human rights policy was strongly influenced by these considerations. Thus, the administration was accused of being "notably and properly articulate and outspoken with regard to the suppression of the rights of labor and the rights of opponents of the present Polish Government, but not so notably voluble with regard to the same groups in Turkey." This lack of evenhandedness was traced to the fact that Turkey was a "much desired partner in NATO" while Poland was "more friendly to the Soviet Union than to the United States." A similar selectivity was seen to be present in the contrasting attitudes taken by the United States in regard to two Western Hemispheric situations marked by an absence of freedom: Nicaragua, about which the United States expressed great concern, and Chile, which was treated more leniently. And, as a final example, Secretary of State Shultz was charged with "underscoring U.S. indifference to the plight of Pakistanis by remaining silent about violations of their rights while championing those of Afghan refugees in Pakistan, to whom he pledged support."[89]

The Reagan administration in these cases demonstrated the impact of not only political/security considerations on the implementation of human rights policy but also of the "authoritarian/totalitarian" dichotomy expressed by Jeane Kirkpatrick:

There are no grounds to expect radical totalitarian regimes to transform themselves. [There is a] far greater likelihood of progressive liberation in Brazil, Argentina, and Chile than in Cuba; in Taiwan than China; South Korea than North Korea; and Zaire than Angola.

Secretary Shultz later concurred:

In the last decade we have seen several military regimes and dictatorships of the right evolve into democracies—from Portugal, Spain, and Greece to Turkey and Argentina. No Communist state has evolved in such manner, though Poland attempted to.

The validity of the "authoritarian/totalitarian" dichotomy as a sound basis for action in the name of a human rights policy has been challenged. One critic of this premise, for example, observed that "distinguishing between totalitarian and authoritarian regimes may have a place in the history classroom, but . . . [not] in the making of foreign policy." Another criticism centers on the administration's contention that authoritarian systems should be treated differently from the totalitarian because of the former's greater potential for becoming democratic. This argument and the examples from history cited in support of it are said to suffer from a fundamental flaw: a superficial definition of "democracy" that views this concept within the limited range of the political culture of the United States.

Democracy is treated in its narrowest sense only, defined as a system of periodic, competitive elections—a definition without standing in international law. International law suggests no reason why the holding of elections per se should be placed on a higher plane of importance than the rights that elections are intended to protect and enhance—be those the right not to be assassinated, the right not to be abducted and not to "disappear", the right not to be tortured, or any of a host of other rights basic to civilized humanity. In practice elections in much of the world do not necessarily guarantee a democratic society or many basic human rights. But the [Reagan] administration's logic insists on defining the prerequisites for human rights primarily in terms of Western-style democratic forms—not always the same as democratic control—rather than in terms of actual conditions of life.[90]

Later years of the Reagan administration saw some changes in its treatment of certain human rights situations. Thus, for example, the 1985–1986 period witnessed a hardening of the administration's approach to the problem of apartheid in South Africa and to the Philippines, where the demise of dictator Marcos was attributed, in part, to the withdrawal of U.S. support for him. Opinions will obviously differ as to whether these shifts reflected a sincere concern for human rights and a determination to be evenhanded in dealing with various human rights situations or simply expedient responses to political realities and pressures, both foreign and domestic.

SUMMARY

The conceptual frameworks within which the human rights foreign policies of the Carter and Reagan administrations were formed contained both common and dissimilar elements. Each administration professed to be including human rights in this country's foreign policy for two reasons: because it was the right thing to do, and because doing so would serve the nation's interests. Both administrations, moreover, placed human rights policy formulation within the context of global political/security considerations, though this factor was more explicit in the Reagan administration than that of Jimmy Carter. The Reagan rationale for a human rights policy also differed from Carter's in its heavy emphasis on the struggle with communism, which was seen as the arch enemy of human rights.

Both administrations had the same system of policy priorities in the sense that both subordinated human rights to national security interests and demands. At the same time, both sought to dull the edge of priorities conflict by asserting a symmetry, or compatibility, between these two. The two administrations differed, though, in that a high priority for human rights was a Carter characteristic from the beginning of his tenure in office, but was not present in the initial stages of Reagan's. A possible further difference between the two could be that, while Carter's assigning a high place to human rights was a matter of conscious, deliberate choice, in Reagan's case the later elevation of human rights was a product of circumstances and pressures.

In their definition of human rights there was a clear difference between the Carter and Reagan administrations since the Carter administration included economic/social rights in its definition but Reagan's did not.

The objectives of the human rights policies of the two administrations, as officially stated, were essentially the same: a mixture of humanitarian and pragmatic purposes. The humanitarian goal was the improvement of the quality of life for people through an improvement in human rights conditions throughout the world, while the pragmatic objective was to serve and protect American political/security interests globally. Since this latter objective was seen as requiring the projection of a favorable image of the United States, a subsidiary purpose of the human rights policies was to disassociate this country from abusive regimes.

In the selection of targets for U.S. actions in defense of human rights, the two were similar in that both were officially committed to dealing in an evenhanded manner with all human rights violations, wherever they occurred. The two differed, however, in the impression they created as to the extent to which evenhandedness actually controlled implementary action. Thus the Carter administration was variously accused of dealing selectively with abusive regimes at both ends of the political spectrum, a fact that suggests more, rather than less, evenhandedness in the administration's approach to human rights situations. The Reagan administration, however, was perceived as being more tolerant of rights violations committed by right-wing dictators who were friendly to the United States than it was of the abuses perpetrated by left-wing regimes who were viewed as hostile to this country. Here, though, as in other aspects of the Reagan human rights policy, there were some indications of a shift in the later years of the administration's life: in this case, toward a sterner stand against abuses committed by some friendly but authoritarian regimes.

NOTES

1. Two other reasons for building human rights into U.S. foreign policy are humanitarian and legal: saving lives and/or improving living conditions, and legis-

lation. The first is not discussed here because it is obvious and present in both administrations, and the second is dealt with in Chapter 3.

2. David Heaps, *Human Rights and U.S. Foreign Policy: The First Decade, 1973–1983* (New York: American Association for the International Commission of Jurists, 1984), pp. 16–17 (hereafter cited as *Human Rights: The First Decade*).

3. U.S. Congress, House of Representatives, Committee on Foreign Affairs, *Human Rights and U.S. Foreign Policy: Hearings Before the Subcommittee on International Organizations*, 96th Cong., 1st Sess., May 2, 10; June 21; July 12; and August 2, 1979, p. 223.

4. Zbigniew Brzezinski, *Power and Principle*, rev. ed. (New York: Farrar, Straus, and Giroux, 1985), p. 81.

5. Cyrus R. Vance, *Hard Choices: Critical Years in America's Foreign Policy* (New York: Simon and Schuster, 1983), pp. 29, 421.

6. Patricia Derian, "The MacNeil/Lehrer Report," Public Broadcasting System, February 10, 1981.

7. Brzezinski, *Power and Principle*, p. 124.

8. *Human Rights: The First Decade*, p. 21.

9. Derian, "MacNeil/Lehrer Report."

10. For the Laquer and Lefever comments, see Derian, "MacNeil/Lehrer Report," and U.S. Congress, *Human Rights and U.S. Foreign Policy*, pp. 224, 227, 229, 240.

11. The Muskie and Derian observations were made in addresses given, respectively, October 21, 1980, at the University of Wisconsin at Milwaukee, and June 13, 1980, in Milwaukee.

12. U.S. Department of State, *Country Reports on Human Rights Practices for 1982: Report Submitted to the Committee on Foreign Affairs, House of Representatives and the Committee on Foreign Relations, U.S. Senate* (Washington, D.C.: U.S. Government Printing Office, 1983), p. 7; and Idem., *Country Reports . . . 1981* (Washington, D.C.: U.S. Government Printing Office, 1982), p. 9.

13. Cynthia Brown, ed., *With Friends Like These*, The Americas Watch Report on Human Rights and U.S. Policy in Latin America (New York: Pantheon Books, 1985), p. 239.

14. Patricia Derian in conversation with the author, September 1985.

15. Joseph Eldridge, Washington Office on Latin America, in personal conversation, September 1985.

16. Address given in Washington, D.C., October 12, 1983.

17. Personal conversations at the Department of State, October 1984.

18. U.S. Department of State, *Country Reports . . . 1981*, p. 9.

19. Arthur M. Schlesinger, Jr., quoted by Jerome Shestack, in U.S. Congress, House of Representatives, Committee on Foreign Affairs, *Political Killings by Governments of Their Citizens: Hearings Before the Subcommittee on Human Rights and International Organizations*, 98th Cong., 1st Sess., November 16 and 17, 1983 (Washington, D.C.: U.S. Government Printing Office, 1983), p. 215.

20. David Carliner, in U.S. Congress, House of Representatives, Committee on Foreign Affairs, *Review of U.S. Human Rights Policy: Hearings Before the Subcommittee on Human Rights and International Organizations*, 98th Cong., 1st Sess., March 3, June 28, September 21, 1983 (Washington, D.C.: U.S. Government Printing Office, 1983), p. 48.

21. Americas Watch, Helsinki Watch, Lawyers Committee for International Human Rights, *The Reagan Administration's Human Rights Policy: A Mid-Term Review* (New York and Washington, D.C.: Author, 1982), p. 4 (hereafter cited as *Mid-Term Review*).

22. Bruce P. Cameron, in U.S. Congress, *Human Rights and U.S. Foreign Policy*, p. 254.

23. David Carleton and Michael Stohl, "The Foreign Policy of Human Rights: Rhetoric and Reality from Jimmy Carter to Ronald Reagan," *Human Rights Quarterly* no. 2 (May 1985): 223f.

24. Vance, *Hard Choices*, p. 33.

25. Ibid., p. 46.

26. Donald L. Ranard, in Caleb Rossiter, *Human Rights: The Carter Record, the Reagan Reaction*, International Policy Report (Washington, D.C.: Center for International Policy, 1984), p. 1.

27. U.S. Congress, House of Representatives, Committee on Foreign Affairs, *Human Rights in Asia: Non-Communist Countries: Hearings Before the Subcommittees on Asian and Pacific Affairs and on International Organizations*, 96th Cong., 2d sess., February 4, 6 and 7, 1980 (Washington, D.C.: U.S. Government Printing Office, 1980), p. 182.

28. Ibid, p. 173. The other means included private diplomatic representations, symbolic public acts, review of aid programs, and a ban on the export of police equipment.

29. U.S. Congress, *Human Rights and U.S. Foreign Policy*, pp. 30–31.

30. Charles W. Freeman, in U.S. Congress, *Human Rights in Asia: Communist Countries: Hearing Before the Subcommittees on Asian and Pacific Affairs and on International Organizations*, 96th Cong., 2d Sess., October 1, 1980 (Washington, D.C.: U.S. Government Printing Office, 1980), p. 48.

31. Donald L. Ranard, in U.S. Congress, *Human Rights in Asia: Non-Communist Countries*, pp. 333f.

32. Patricia Derian, quoted in V. Aksyonov, "Overhaul U.S. Human Rights Policy?" *U.S. News and World Report*, March 2, 1981, p. 50.

33. Benedict O'Gorman Anderson, in U.S. Congress, *Human Rights in Asia: Non-Communist Countries*, pp. 232, 244.

34. Raul Manglapus, in U.S. Congress, House of Representatives, Committee on Foreign Affairs, *Human Rights in the Philippines: Hearing Before the Subcommittee*, 98th Cong., 1st Sess., September 22, 1983 (Washington, D.C.: U.S. Government Printing Office, 1983), p. 17.

35. Edward J. Derwinski, in U.S. Congress, *Human Rights and U.S. Foreign Policy*, p. 116.

36. Stanley J. Heginbotham, in Ibid., p. 348.

37. *Human Rights: The First Decade*, p. 26.

38. Stephen Cohen, "Conditioning U.S. Security Assistance on Human Rights Practices", *American Journal of International Law* 76 (January-April 1982): 270.

39. Michael T. Klare and Cynthia Arnson, *Supplying Repression: U.S. Support for Authoritarian Regimes Abroad*, rev. ed. (Washington, D.C.: Institute for Policy Studies, 1981), p. 85, and William Goodfellow, Center for International Policy Studies, conversation with the author, May 1985.

40. *The New York Times*, January 13, 1981.

41. Bzrezinski, *Power and Principle*, p. 49.

42. Derian and Schneider, conversations with the author, May and September 1985.

43. U.S. Congress, *Human Rights and U.S. Foreign Policy*, pp. 163, 184.

44. Bzrezinski, *Power and Principle*, p. 397, U.S. Congress, *Human Rights and U.S. Foreign Policy*, p. 472, Vance, *Hard Choices*, p. 46; Brown, *With Friends Like These*, pp. 92, 99, 180, 193.

45. U.S. Congress, *Human Rights and U.S. Foreign Policy*, p. 16.

46. Richard L. Feinberg, *U.S. Human Rights Policy: Latin America*, International Policy Report (Washington, D.C.: Center for International Policy, 1980), p. 2. The same point is made by Carleton and Stohl, "The Foreign Policy of Human Rights," p. 224.

47. Carleton and Stohl, "The Foreign Policy of Human Rights," p. 224.

48. Aksyonov, "Overhaul of U.S. Human Rights Policy?"

49. Address in Washington, D.C., March 31, 1981, and news conference January 28, 1981.

50. U.S. Department of State, *Country Reports . . . for 1981*, p. 9.

51. *Human Rights: The First Decade*, pp. 31, 33.

52. Juan de Onis, "Administration Courting Four South American Regimes," *Louisville Courier-Journal*, March 8, 1981; "Reagan Off to a Shaky Start with Human Rights Policy," *Louisville Courier-Journal*, March 11, 1981; U.S. Congress, *Review of U.S. Human Rights Policy*, p. 86; and R. Gregory Nokes, "Human Rights Take Backseat to War on Communism," *Indianapolis Star*, February 22, 1981.

53. Department of State official, personal conversation, September 1985.

54. Joseph Eldridge, personal conversation, September 1985.

55. Coalition for a New Foreign and Military Policy, *The Reagan Administration: Human Rights Under Attack*, Coalition Close-up (Washington, D.C.: Coalition, 1981).

56. Comment by an associate of the Center for International Policy, personal conversation, May 1985.

57. This discussion is based on *Human Rights: The First Decade*, pp. 35–37.

58. Ibid., pp. 35–37, and conversations at the Department of State, October 1984 and September 1985.

59. Brown, *With Friends Like These*, pp. 132 and 240.

60. Americas Watch, Helsinki Watch, Lawyers Committee for International Human Rights, *Failure: The Reagan Administration's Human Rights Policy in 1983* (New York and Washington, D.C.: Author, 1984), pp. 52–55 (hereafter cited as *Failure*).

61. Ibid., pp. 30, 44, 70; and Americas Watch, Helsinki Watch, Lawyers Committee for International Human Rights, *In the Face of Cruelty: The Reagan Administration's Human Rights Record in 1984*, pp. 77–78 (hereafter cited as *In the Face of Cruelty*).

62. U.S. Congress, *Review of U.S. Human Rights Policy*. p. 151, and U.S. Congress, House of Representatives, Committee on Foreign Affairs, *The Phenomenon of Torture: Hearings and Markup Before the Subcommittee on Human Rights and International Organizations*, 98th Cong., 2d Sess., May 15 and 16 and September 6, 1984 (Washington, D.C.: U.S. Government Printing Office, 1984), p. 155.

63. Lawyers Committee for Human Rights and The Watch Committees, *The Reagan Administration's Record on Human Rights in 1985* (New York and Washington, D.C.: Author, 1986), p. 1.

64. *Failure*, p. 34; and U.S. Congress, *Review of U.S. Human Rights Policy*, pp.

5–6.

65. Brown, *With Friends Like These*, p. 199.

66. Ibid., pp. 206, 241.

67. *In the Face of Cruelty*, p. 90.

68. Ibid., pp. 105–106.

69. Ibid., pp. 59–61.

70. Jo Marie Greisgraber, in U.S. Congress, *Human Rights and U.S. Foreign Policy*, p. 149; and *Human Rights: The First Decade*, p. 50.

71. Quoted in A. Glenn Mower, Jr., *The United States, the United Nations, and Human Rights* (Westport, Conn.: Greenwood Press, 1979), p. 91.

72. *Human Rights: The First Decade*, p. 49.

73. U.S. Congress, *Human Rights and U.S. Foreign Policy*, p. 23.

74. U.S. Congress, *Human Rights in Asia: Communist Countries*, p. 27.

75. U.S. Department of State, *Country Reports . . . for 1981*, p. 6.

76. Conversations at the Department of State, October 1984.

77. U.S. Department of State, *Country Reports . . . for 1985*, pp. 1–2. Workers' rights are included in the International Covenant on Economic, Social, and Cultural Rights (UN) and the European Social Charter (Council of Europe) and thus clearly belong in the category of economic/social rights, which is absent from the Reagan administration's definition of human rights. For a description and analysis of the Covenant and the Charter, see A. Glenn Mower, Jr., *International Cooperation for Social Justice* (Westport, Conn.: Greenwood Press, 1985).

78. This description of the objectives of the Carter administration's human rights policy is based on Brzezinski, *Power and Principle*, pp. 54, 126; "The MacNeil/Lehrer Report"; conversations at the Department of State, September 1985; Edmund Muskie, address at the University of Wisconsin/Milwaukee; and President Carter's legislative message to the 2nd session of the 96th Congress, 1980.

79. This discussion of the objectives of the Reagan administration's human rights policy is based on conversations at the Department of State, October 1984; U.S. Department of State, *Country Reports . . . for 1982*, p. 7; U.S. Congress, *Review of U.S. Human Rights Policy*, p. 151; U.S. Department of State, *Human Rights and Foreign Policy*, Department of State Selected Documents No. 22 (Washington, D.C.: U.S. Government Printing Office, 1983); and U.S. Department of State, *1984 Human Rights Report*, Department of State Special Report no. 121 (Washington, D.C.: U.S. Government Printing Office, 1985).

80. The point of possible complicity is made in Klare and Arnson, *Supplying Repression*, pp. 3–7.

81. The preceding discussion of selectivity under the Carter administration is based on Ibid., p. 85; U.S. Department of State, *Human Rights in Asia: Non-Communist Countries*, p. 89; U.S. Department of State, *Human Rights in Asia: Communist Countries*, pp. 128–129; Cohen, "Conditioning U.S. Security Assistance on Human Rights Practices," p. 128; and U.S. Congress, *Human Rights and U.S. Foreign Policy*, pp. 186, 235.

82. The sources for this and the preceding paragraph are U.S. Congress, *Human Rights in Asia: Communist Countries*, p. 34; U.S. Congress, *Human Rights and U.S. Foreign Policy*, pp. 308, 338, 344, and New York address by Patricia Derian, April 24, 1980.

83. The sources for these expressions of the Reagan policy are U.S. Department

of State, *Human Rights and the Moral Dimension of U.S. Foreign Policy*, Current Policy no. 551 (Washington, D.C.: U.S. Government Printing Office, 1984), p. 3; U.S. Department of State, *Country Reports . . . for 1981*, p. 9; and U.S. Congress, *Review of U.S. Human Rights Policy*, p. 9.

84. *Human Rights: The First Decade*, p. 42.

85. *Mid-Term Review*, p. 1; and U.S. Congress, *Review of U.S. Human Rights Policy*, pp. 50–51.

86. U.S. Congress, *The Phenomenon of Torture*, p. 185.

87. *The New York Times*, August 27 and October 25, 1985.

88. Ibid, May 8, 1985.

89. U.S. Congress, *Review of U.S. Human Rights Policy*, pp. 36–37, and *Failure*, p. 50.

90. Jeane Kirkpatrick, "Dictatorships and Double Standards," *Commentary*, November 1979, p. 44; George Shultz, in U.S. Department of State, *Human Rights and the Moral Dimension*, p. 4; Jeri Laber, in U.S. Congress, *Review of U.S. Human Rights Policy*, p. 92; Brown, *With Friends Like These*, p. 9.

3

The Sources of the Human Rights Policies

We turn now to the sources of Carter's and Reagan's policies, the influences that were at work when these policies were being developed. They were of two types: legal and political.

The legal factors included international agreements and national laws. From these sources came certain obligations to act on behalf of human rights, and, in some cases, prescriptions as to the nature of these actions.

The political sources of human rights policies for both administrations included the national bureaucracy and Congress, both of which had some impact on what each administration did in respect to human rights.

How these two types of influences affected the human rights policies of the Carter and Reagan administrations, and how these administrations reacted to them, is the subject of this chapter.

LEGAL SOURCES OF HUMAN RIGHTS POLICIES: INTERNATIONAL

One factor common to both the Carter and Reagan administrations was the obligation assumed by this country under international law to encourage respect for human rights throughout the world.

This obligation is recognized in Section 502B of the Foreign Assistance Act of 1961, as amended, part of which states:

The United States shall, in accordance with its international obligations as set forth in the Charter of the United Nations . . . promote and encourage increased respect for human rights and fundamental freedoms throughout the world. . . . Accordingly, a principal goal of the foreign policy of the United States shall be to promote the increased observance of internationally recognized human rights by all countries.[1]

The international obligations to which this act refers include the pledge made by all members when they join the UN, "to take joint and separate action . . . for the achievement of the purposes set forth in Article 55" (Article 56). Included in Article 55 is the goal of promoting "universal respect for and observance of human rights and fundamental freedoms for all." That the United States through its membership in the UN assumed this obligation effectively refutes the allegation made, for example, by Ernest W. Lefever, that "in a formal and legal sense the U.S. Government has no responsibility— and certainly no authority—to promote human rights in other sovereign states."[2]

International human rights law also includes a host of conventions, covenants, and other agreements, which could also be said to obligate the United States to incorporate the promotion and defense of human rights in its foreign policy. In support of this contention it has been argued that these agreements have become part of customary international law, giving them meaning even for those countries that have not adhered to specific agreements. Customary international law has been upheld in the courts. In 1980, for example, a U.S. appeals court ruled that a former Paraguayan police officer emigrating to the United States could be sued in U.S. courts for his alleged torture killing in Paraguay, since international agreements and declarations had become part of customary international law and "official torture is now prohibited by the law of nations."[3]

Under the obligations of international human rights law the United States must not only encourage respect for human rights throughout the world, but, as Stephen B. Cohen suggests, it must also refrain from supporting any government that is guilty of serious violations of internationally recognized human rights.[4]

When an American administration incorporates human rights in its foreign policy, it is thus carrying out its responsibilities under international law. The fact that the purpose of this policy is to protect and promote internationally recognized human rights constitutes an effective reply to those who see a U.S. human rights policy as "an attempt to impose unilateral standards on the rest of the world."[5]

The Carter Administration

The Carter administration acknowledged its obligation under international human rights agreements and declarations to work for the advancement of human rights.[6] This administration also sought to strengthen the impact of these international instruments on U.S. foreign policy by urging U.S. ratification of five human rights treaties. One of these pacts, the American Convention on Human Rights, was the work of the Organization of American States, while the other four had their source in the UN: the Genocide

Convention, the Convention on Racial Discrimination, and the Covenants on Economic, Social, and Cultural Rights and on Civil and Political Rights.

While the Genocide Convention was already before the Senate for its consent to ratification, Carter's signing and submission of the other four treaties was an initiative of his administration. If Carter had succeeded in gaining Senate consent to their ratification, the United States would have become a participant in the treaties' supervisory proceedings, which would mean direct injection of human rights into this country's dealings with other countries. As a party to these agreements, moreover, the United States would be in a stronger position, morally and politically, to pursue a vigorous policy vis-à-vis governments with questionable human rights records. Finally, by becoming a party to these treaties, the United States would have another means of gaining information concerning human rights conditions in other countries and attitudes of particular governments about these conditions. Such information could influence the direction, substance, and intensity of U.S. human rights foreign policy.

The Carter administration thus not only accepted the fact that international law imposed obligations on this country to act on behalf of human rights, but it acted to increase the scope of these obligations and strengthen the impact of international human rights instruments on U.S. foreign policy.

The ratification of these five major international human rights treaties was one of the Carter administration's major foreign policy goals.[7] However, the administration failed to win the Senate's cooperation in removing what Assistant Secretary of State Warren Christopher called "a problem for the United States in its human rights diplomacy": American nonadherence to these agreements.[8] Some commentators attribute this failure to the president's "lack of push for the Senate's . . . consent" when he submitted the treaties. There was, according to this opinion, a "gap between the [President's] human rights rhetoric and his willingness to spend political capital" in order to reach some human rights objectives, including the ratification of the human rights treaties. One observer professed to see an example of this in Carter's handling of the Genocide Convention. He made an "eloquent plea" on its behalf but then made "no effort to corral the necessary number of Senators to even vote cloture" and thus insure debate and vote on the Convention.[9]

One effort the Carter administration did make to gain Senate consent to ratification of the human rights treaties it submitted was to propose a number of reservations to be attached to U.S. adherence to these agreements. These reservations were prepared in anticipation of the objections senators could be expected to make to these treaties and hence were a significant part of the campaign to make the U.S. a party to the treaties.[10]

Despite this effort, the Carter administration failed to win Senate consent to ratification. This failure may be attributed as much to the inherent difficulties of winning Senate approval for any major treaty as to the alleged absence of administration pressure on the Senate. The intense conflicts in the Senate over other treaties sent there by the Carter administration—notably SALT II and the Panama Canal Treaty—testify to the extent of the difficulties of the treaty-ratification process.

The Reagan Administration

International instruments comprised one of the sources of the human rights foreign policy of the Reagan administration. Thus, in the words of one of its spokespersons,

Together with our Bill of Rights and Declaration of Independence, the UN Charter and the Universal Declaration of Human Rights form the basis for U.S. human rights policy. The UN documents constitute a legal commitment by almost all governments to respect human rights, and this is the justification for our approaches to governments . . . regarding their human rights practices.

Moreover, according to this source, the fact that these international instruments, plus the Helsinki Final Act, form the basis of U.S. human rights policy is evidence that "we do not seek to impose American institutions or methods on other countries."[11] The Reagan administration's human rights policy may indeed have international human rights instruments as a source. However, it has not always been so perceived as indicated by the following observation:

Rarely does a spokesman for this administration invoke the Universal Declaration of Human Rights in voicing concern about human rights abuses. Rarely can one find in official statements mention of any of the international declarations or treaties which form the legal foundation of international concern and action.[12]

Whatever skepticism exists concerning the role that international human rights agreements played in the shaping of the Reagan administration's foreign policy is quite likely a result of the negative attitude that it has taken toward such instruments over the years. Reagan's first nominee for the position of head of the Human Rights Bureau, Ernest W. Lefever, for example, wondered "why we should feel compelled to sign this Genocide treaty"[13]; and his administration was accused by one State department official of failing to promote human rights covenants as zealously as did its predecessor.[14] The same judgement was pronounced by a 1986 study, which noted that the Reagan administration "continued to withhold support for four principal human rights treaties, all signed but not ratified by the U.S.": the two major UN Covenants, the UN Convention on Racial Discrimination, and the American Convention on Human Rights.[15] This record of nonsupport for U.S. ratification of human rights treaties was compiled under a president who has been described as being uniquely qualified to get them accepted: a judgment based on the fact that Reagan's political support came mainly from those who could be expected to oppose American adherence to these treaties.[16]

The Reagan administration's apparent unwillingness to push for acceptance of a number of major human rights pacts was somewhat counterbalanced by its positive attitude toward the Conventions on Genocide and Torture. Thus, Reagan's support was seen as "the crucial factor" in the Senate's favorable action on the Genocide Convention in 1986. He had announced in 1984 that he supported ratification, and in 1985 he sent a letter to Majority Leader Robert Dole, urging Senate action on the convention.[17] Concerning the Convention on Torture, Human Rights Bureau head Elliott Abrams testified in 1984 that the United States would support this treaty when it came before the UN General Assembly.[18]

LEGAL SOURCES OF HUMAN RIGHTS POLICIES: NATIONAL LAWS

Under a series of laws enacted by the U.S. Congress, the Carter and Reagan administrations were mandated to incorporate human rights in this country's foreign policy. This legislation originated in the early 1970s when Congress became dissatisfied with the foreign policies of the Nixon and Ford administrations. A major cause of congressional concern was the association of this country with two regimes considered to be serious violators of human rights: those in South Vietnam and Chile. This linkage prompted a series of hearings on the relationship between human rights and U.S. foreign policy, conducted by the Subcommittee on International Organizations and Movements of the House Foreign Affairs Committee, presided over by Donald M. Fraser. These hearings led, in 1974, to the first elements in what has become a considerable body of legislation designed to achieve two major objectives: the promotion of human rights abroad and the dissociation of the United States from repressive regimes.

Congressional action included a call for the establishment of a human rights office in the State Department, a mandate for annual State Department reports on human rights practices in other countries, and, dating from 1974, a series of resolutions and laws that have made certain U.S. aid programs subject to human rights conditions. A major piece of legislation was the 1976 amendment to Section 502B of the Foreign Assistance Act of 1961, in which Congress issued a clear prescription for a foreign policy that would include human rights. The amendment (1) posited the promotion of the increased observance of internationally recognized human rights as a principal goal of U.S. foreign policy, (2) stipulated that, except under specified circumstances, no security assistance is to be provided for any country whose government engages in a consistent pattern of gross violations of internationally recognized human rights, and (3) stated that international security assistance programs are to be so formulated as to promote and advance human rights and avoid the identification of the United States with governments that deny internationally recognized human rights to their people.

Human rights provisions were also written into legislation governing non-military, nonsecurity assistance programs. An amendment to Section 112 of the Agricultural Trade Development and Assistance Act of 1954, for example, forbade any agreement to finance the sale of agricultural commodities to the government of any country where internationally recognized human rights are consistently violated.

As a result of legislative activity since the early 1970s, by 1983 there were fifty-four specific pieces of legislation in this field, under nine categories: the Foreign Assistance Act of 1961 as amended, the Arms Export Control Act, the Agricultural Trade Development and Assistance Act of 1954 as amended, legislation dealing with international financial institutions, the Bretton Woods Agreement Act as amended, the Export-Import Bank Act of 1945 as amended, the Trade Act of 1974, State Department and Foreign Relations Authorization Acts of 1982 and 1983 and for 1979, and Country Specific Provisions relating to twelve nations. Of the fifty-four specific enactments, twenty-six contain general policy statements, and twenty impose certain prohibitions and/or restrictions.[19] These laws were enacted with the clear intention of affecting the way administrations formulate and implement this country's foreign policy. Whether or not this purpose is realized in actual practice depends on a number of variables.

The most significant variable factor affecting the impact of human rights legislation on U.S. foreign policy is, of course, the attitude of the administration in office toward these laws. As Stephen Cohen points out,

Inevitably there is a gap between legislation and execution, especially when the Executive is not wholly sympathetic to the law. The gap may even devour legislated policies as the Executive refuses "to take care that the laws be faithfully executed," and bureaucratic and personal considerations distort judgments, exploit the generality and uncertainty of language, and lead to abuse of discretion.[20]

The capacity of any administration to determine the real effectiveness of human rights legislation cannot be questioned; it is certainly true that, in Congressman Donald Fraser's words, "If you have an administration that doesn't care about human rights, . . . it will be very hard to compel them to be interested no matter what you write into the statutory language."[21]

The "statutory language" itself is a factor that enables any administration to evade or negate a human rights law, if it is so minded. By political necessity or a desire to avoid undue rigidity, the authors of human rights legislation included certain provisions that can be used as escape hatches by administrations unwilling to apply the law in specific situations. Thus Section 116(a) of the Foreign Assistance Act prohibits aid to rights violators unless this assistance will directly benefit the needy people of the country in question. A similar loophole exists in the legislation (Section 502B, Foreign Assistance Act) that bans military assistance to gross violators of human rights; exceptions are permitted under "extraordinary circumstances" involving American national security interests.

Imperfect though they are as mandates binding on administrations, the human rights laws enacted in a succession of congressional sessions constitute a framework within which administrations must operate as they develop their foreign policies and a constant reminder that the law of the land dictates that human rights must be considered when this policy is formed and carried out. The response of the Carter and Reagan administrations to this body of human rights legislation is the subject of the following discussion.

The Carter Administration

The official position of the Carter administration concerning human rights laws, according to Human Rights Bureau head Patricia Derian, was that this legislation was "the foundation of its human rights policy." Carter's deputy assistant secretary of state, Warren Christopher, made a similar assertion when he testified to a congressional subcommittee that "we are committed to carrying out the letter and the spirit of these laws."[22]

This commitment to applying human rights laws did not, however, produce a perfect performance record. Thus, Stephen Cohen's review of this record, with particular reference to the Carter administration's approach to Section 502B of the Foreign Assistance Act, led him to observe that:

In some instances the Carter Administration adopted a highly strained reading of the statute which, although not contrary to its literal terms, produced a result contrary to Congressional intent. In other cases the language was simply disregarded, so that decisions violated even the letter of the law.[23]

Criticism of the Carter administration's behavior in respect to human rights laws charged that "even while adhering to the letter of the law, agencies of the federal government" had certainly "gone against the spirit of human rights policy, . . . acting against the intent of human rights legislation by stretching loopholes beyond any common sense definition."[24]

Administrative abuse of the "extraordinary circumstances/national security interest" loopholes was seen, for example, in the decision to provide military aid to South Korea and the Philippines despite their poor human rights records.[25] Indonesia was another situation where security assistance was provided despite an alleged failure by the Carter administration to "make a case" that extraordinary circumstances existed that would justify this action.[26]

The Carter administration was also accused of taking undue advantage of another loophole in human rights legislation: the "basic human needs" exception to the law against economic assistance to countries where repressive regimes were in control. Thus it was alleged that "all AID loans [were] billed as meeting basic human needs" without "an assessment of the overall policy of the recipient government in its treatment of its own people."[27]

While the Carter administration's performance in regard to human rights laws was not above negative criticism, all in all, in the opinion of one observer, this administration "viewed the [human rights] legislative framework as an authorization for more human rights activity [and] to a great extent implemented the Congressional will that human rights be made an important factor in U.S. foreign policy."[28] A similarly favorable assessment of the Carter administration's attitude toward human rights laws, by Stephen Cohen, noted that "it should be obvious from the record that the Carter Administration did much more than its predecessors to implement Section 502B [of the Foreign Assistance Act]." In support of his conclusion, Cohen pointed to some specific steps taken by this administration:

1. Human rights were given a hearing at nearly all stages of the decision-making process concerning military aid and arms sales.
2. The Bureau of Human Rights was given a "reasonably full opportunity" to make its views known through action memorandums.
3. Sales of new weapons were banned to eight Latin American countries, and, with few exceptions, these countries were given little or no military aid in the 1978–1981 period.[29]

While the Carter administration was accused of frustrating the intent of human rights laws by its resort to the loopholes, the invoking of these exceptions was also seen as a legitimate exercise of executive prerogative. The Carter administration obviously used this prerogative on numerous occasions: in the cases of a loan to Paraguay, seen as actually helping needy people, and aid to Turkey, on security grounds, for example.[30] In view of the highly subjective nature of such terms as "needy people," "extraordinary circumstance," and "national security interests," opinions will obviously vary as to whether or not these and other exercises of administrative prerogative were justified.

The Reagan Administration

One early assessment of the Reagan administration's human rights policy, commenting on its faithfulness in executing human rights laws, concluded that "the Reagan Administration's approach to these laws differed sharply from both the Ford and Carter Administrations." That this comparison was not favorable to the Reagan administration is indicated by another conclusion reached through this review: that this administration had "openly disregarded many of the laws governing human rights policy."[31]

A similar analysis of the Reagan administration's performance in regard to human rights legislation two years later returned the same negative verdict, alleging that "in 1983 the Reagan Administration continued to ignore, re-define, veto, or defy U.S. laws governing human rights policy. . . . From the outset the Reagan Administration has defied the intent of these laws."[32] When the administration's human rights record for 1985 was reviewed, the conclusion again was that the administration "continued to flout, circumvent, or bend the meaning of a number of human rights laws to serve its political objectives."[33] These negative evaluations of the Reagan administration in regard to human rights laws were based on what was perceived to be failures to implement this legislation in a number of specific cases, of which the following are examples.

1. Guatemala. Early in its tenure in office the administration removed trucks and jeeps from the list of items considered security assistance and then approved the sale to Guatemala of this equipment, despite this country's poor human rights record. This tactic prompted criticism that the administration was "openly ig-noring" the law banning such assistance to countries with poor human rights records.

2. El Salvador. Another country judged to be guilty of serious rights violations, El Salvador was repeatedly certified by the Reagan administration to be eligible for military assistance.

3. Pakistan. The administration in 1981 concluded a six-year military and economic aid agreement in spite of reports of the Pakistani government's mistreatment of political prisoners and in apparent disregard of Section 620E of the Foreign As-sistance Act, which stipulated that the aid was to be used "to promote the ex-peditious restoration of full civil liberties and representative government in Pakistan."

4. South Korea. In 1983 the administration supported loans for South Korea despite restrictions of the International Financial Institutions Act.

5. The Philippines. The national police force received U.S. aid even though Section 660 of the Foreign Assistance Act prohibited direct U.S. aid to any personnel with internal law enforcement responsibilities.

6. Haiti. In 1985, the administration declared Haiti to be eligible for General System of Preferences status despite charges that Haiti violated labor standards contained in the trade legislation, renewed in 1984, that established this system. Under this law, only those countries complying with the enumerated norms were to be accorded preferential treatment.[34] Negative appraisals of the administration's at-titude toward human rights laws were also inspired by its willingness to resort to loopholes in this legislation in order to justify the extension of aid to countries with poor human rights records. Thus Haiti was declared eligible for aid on the grounds that there had been a significant improvement in Haiti's human rights situation. The administration was thus invoking that provision within Section 502B of the Foreign Assistance Act of 1961, as amended, which states that aid may be supplied to a country if the president finds that this country has significantly improved its human rights record.[35]

Another case illustrating the Reagan Administration's resort to loopholes in human rights laws involved Ethiopia, in respect to which Congress had mandated a trade embargo, an action prompted by that country's poor human rights record. The legislation's implementation, however, depended on a presidential finding that Ethiopia was deliberately starving its people and had failed to grant its citizens fundamental human rights. Despite its harsh criticism of Ethiopia's human rights performance, the administration decided that the country's government was not pursuing a policy of starvation and consequently did not impose the embargo.[36]

A final example of the use of administrative discretion by the Reagan Administration is provided by its use of the phrase "consistent pattern of gross violations of internationally recognized human rights" in legislation governing U.S. aid to other countries. Since "consistent pattern" and "gross violations" have no fixed, universally applicable meaning, these terms must be defined in particular situations. According to administration spokespersons, this power to define has been used not to frustrate but to fulfill the intent of human rights laws. Thus, in testimony to a congressional subcommittee, Human Rights Bureau head Elliott Abrams acknowledged that the existence of a consistent pattern had to be determined in individual situations and that his office played a key role in making this determination. But, according to Abrams, all this was done in a way that "would implement the applicable statutes in a manner consistent with their letter and intent." In further support of his contention Secretary Abrams noted that the administration "pursues a policy of incorporating human rights considerations into assistance programs even in cases where we may not believe that a consistent pattern of gross violations exists." Thus, for example, the bureau might recommend the granting of military aid to a certain country but not providing police equipment or crime control and detection devices.[37] Moreover, when equipment of this kind was supplied to countries guilty of human rights abuses, despite legislation prohibiting such action, "every effort was made to reform the forces receiving [this] aid [and] to eliminate abuses."[38]

As another example of the administration's "commitment to enforcing and going beyond the letter of the law" Abrams called attention to the administration's changing the regulations concerning the exporting of equipment that could be used for crowd-control purposes, to include cattle prods.[39]

The thesis that the Reagan administration did in fact act in ways that would give effect to human rights laws is supported by comments included in various studies of its record. One review noted that the laws governing certification of countries for U.S. aid had been followed and military assistance forbidden in the cases of Chile and Argentina, and that, after initially providing support for Guatemala contrary to human rights legislation, the administration suspended an agreement to sell military spare parts to this country.[40]

POLITICAL SOURCES OF HUMAN RIGHTS POLICIES: THE BUREAUCRACY

Making foreign policy in any substantive field is subject to the powerful influence of the bureaucracy, that part of the governmental structure composed of career officers whose official function is to provide politically neutral support for whatever administration holds office. There are two sides to this support. The first is to supply objective information and advice needed by the political officials, who are, in at least a formal sense, the decision makers. Once decisions have been made, bureaucratic support assumes its second aspect: the implementing of those decisions. The bureaucracy also serves to provide continuity and stability in this country's foreign policy.

The bureaucracy, of course, seldom performs in such an ideal manner because it is not a homogeneous institution, but a collection of agencies, departments, bureaus, and offices. Each of these entities deals with a specific subject or geographical area, and consequently has its own set of interests, concerns, and objectives to promote and protect. Each of these entities, furthermore, has its own status in the total bureaucratic establishment to advance and/or preserve. Consequently, the process of fulfilling the official bureaucratic functions of providing policy guidance and implementation becomes fraught with struggle and conflict. The formulation and implementation of foreign policy are thus greatly conditioned by the dynamics of bureaucratic behavior.

Obviously an examination of the sources of the human rights policies of the Carter and Reagan administrations must include a look at the role of the bureaucracy in determining what place human rights would occupy in their foreign policies. Human rights, like all aspects of foreign policy, is affected by what is called the "bureaucratic perspective."

Bureaucrats will examine any policy proposal, at least in part, to determine whether it will increase the effectiveness with which the mission of their particular organization can be carried out; their organizational responsibilities will help to define the face of the issue they see.[41]

Inevitably the proposal to build a human rights component into U.S. foreign policy was viewed within this bureaucratic perspective and, specifically, within the perspective of the State Department's career bureaucracy, the Foreign Service. Seeing its primary role as being the ensuring of good relations between the United States and the governments of other countries, the Foreign Service reacted negatively to the introduction of an issue like human rights that was likely to disturb these relations.

A point of particular concern to the service, and especially to those members who staffed the five regional bureaus, was Section 502B of the amended

Foreign Assistance Act of 1961. This legislation placed human rights conditions on U.S. aid to other nations, a policy restriction that the service opposed because military aid and arms sales were seen as important means of maintaining cordial relations with other governments. To refuse aid of this kind to another government was seen as a serious threat to good relations, especially when the reason for this refusal was disapproval of the way a regime treated its own people.[42]

Whatever efforts the Carter and Reagan administrations made to incorporate human rights into U.S. foreign policy would thus inevitably be strongly influenced by the bureaucracy's attitude. If the prevailing attitude was that "you don't irritate a government unduly by indicating they are gross violators of human rights," then the formulation and implementation of a human rights policy would be quite difficult.[43] If, on the other hand, the bureaucracy was willing to accept human rights as a legitimate part of the international agenda, then the framing and execution of a policy would be much easier. We turn now to the experiences of the Carter and Reagan administrations.

The Carter Administration

Jimmy Carter's declared intention to make human rights a central focus of his foreign policy precipitated an intense bureaucratic struggle, which greatly affected both the content and the implementation of his administration's human rights policy. What emerged as the Carter human rights policy, in short, was the product of conflict; what the administration had in the way of a human rights policy was what it was able to get from a bureaucracy that contained hostile elements. This antagonism toward a human rights foreign policy was particularly strong early in the Carter administration. Looking back on this period, one of its officials later recalled that this was the time when

we were trying to establish human rights and the realm of law as something we ought to be hearing about. There was perhaps no larger battle than the one that was fought in the bureaucracy. And I want to tell you that it was quite vicious. And there were occasions when Patt [Derian] would confide in her friends how difficult and painful it was.[44]

The harsh fact confronting President Carter and the human rights advocates within his administration was that there was "a relatively thin layer of support for human rights within the State Department. There was strong opposition to the policy . . . at the working level in many parts of the Department."[45]

The Carter human rights policy met particularly stubborn resistance when it involved the implementation of Section 502B of the amended Foreign Assistance Act, barring military aid to human rights violators. This issue brought the Human Rights Bureau, a new addition to the bureaucracy, into direct conflict with career officials who adamantly opposed the new office's attempts to make policy conform to legislation. This opposition involved a number of tactics: (1) arguing that, far from being the controlling factor in the making of any security assistance decision, Section 502B was merely one of a number of policy aspects to be considered; (2) attempting to distort information concerning human rights practices in other countries by issuing reports that minimized the seriousness of abusive practices, on one hand, and that overstated the improvements allegedly being made by the governments in question on the other; and (3) making exaggerated claims concerning the degree to which a given situation affected this country's vital interests and hence the harm that would be done to these interests by a refusal, on human rights grounds, to provide the proposed security assistance.

The strongest resistance to the Human Rights Bureau's efforts came from the State Department's geographic bureaus, principally those dealing with Latin America, East Asia, and Africa. A number of factors combined to produce a relationship that has been described as "contentious, almost uncooperative."[46] As a new agency responsible for promoting a functional concern, the Human Rights Bureau was seen by the regional bureaus as a "turf" invader, attempting to affect policy in geographic areas for which they were traditionally responsible. The regional bureaus' opposition can also be explained in terms of the concept of "clientism": the tendency of career officers to see other governments as "clients," to identify with their interests, and to resent and oppose anything that would disturb smooth, cordial relations with them.

Given this interest in preserving good relations with other governments, and the tendency of governments to resent criticism of the way they handled their internal affairs, it was not surprising that career officers should react negatively to the idea that human rights should be placed on the international agenda. Human rights was thus opposed because it was seen as a potentially disruptive influence. Moreover, the injection of human rights into diplomatic proceedings constituted a major departure from standard practice, one that compelled foreign service personnel to deal with an issue to which little thought had previously been given, and one with which at least some of them were uncomfortable.[47]

Several other factors contributed to this bureaucratic struggle. One was the general tendency of the bureaucracy to resist what it considers to be ill-conceived policy initiatives from the administration. A second contributing factor was the basic incompatibility between the policy views of Patricia Derian, head of the Human Rights Bureau, and those of Richard Holbrooke and Terence Todman, who directed the bureaus responsible for the two regions where human rights problems were particularly acute: East Asia and the Pacific, and Latin America. Commenting on the clash between these personalities, Caleb Rossiter has observed, "Derian's preference for vigorous, uncompromising stands fed Todman's and Holbrooke's similarly uncompromising stands, motivated in part by their protection of their 'turf' and in part by disagreements over policy.''[48]

The personality factor became more critical because some of the participants tended to take the conflict personally. Some individuals were also inclined to overreact to the disagreements that are an inevitable part of the policy-making process.

Another factor underlying the conflict over the Carter human rights policy was the composition of the Human Rights Bureau and the way this office sought to discharge its responsibilities. Some of the conflict could possibly have been avoided had the bureau been headed by a senior foreign service officer, who "might have reduced the new bureau's sense of insecurity and the geographic bureaus' wariness." This kind of appointment, however, was not made, presumably because of Secretary of State Vance's "desire for a fresh perspective for a new policy." The result was the appointment, as head of the Human Rights Bureau, of Patricia Derian, who has been described as "the classic outsider" and whose staff included a significant number of persons who also came from outside the foreign service establishment.[49] It was evident from the moment Patricia Derian assumed the position of assistant secretary of state for human rights and humanitarian affairs that, under her leadership, the Human Rights Bureau would be an active promoter of the cause of human rights. Hence, in Stephen Cohen's words, it would be a "counterweight to the clientism of the regional bureaus."[50] The determination with which Patricia Derian would press for the implementation of human rights legislation stemmed from her view of her role in the Carter administration. She made this view quite clear from the beginning of her official career, for example, in her statement to Deputy Secretary of State Warren Christopher: "If you want a magnolia to decorate foreign policy, I'm the wrong person. I expect to get things done." Her aggressive attitude also came through in her reply to the question of whether she thought she would "win them all": "No, but I expect to win more than I lose."[51] Derian's sense of purpose—"I'm here to make changes and uphold U.S. law"[52]—was bound to put her on a collision course with those in the career service who objected to the changes she had in mind and to any serious attempt to implement human rights legislation. This, in her mind, was a situation that she had to meet not by compromising but by fighting for the policy with which her bureau was entrusted. With the blessing and support of senior State Department personnel, notably Warren Christopher, she waged the battle for a human rights policy priority with a fervor and unwillingness to accept defeat that was frightening to some people in the department. The passionate commitment to the administration's human rights policy that Patricia Derian brought to her position caused some to view her as "too far out," a "wild person," and a "poor loser." Acting on this commitment, she undoubtedly upset some foreign service officers and caused waves in the bureaucracy and in overseas missions. It is quite apparent, however, that someone like her was necessary if the new bureau was to win a place for itself and human rights was to be taken seriously as a foreign policy component. There is a lot of truth in the observation that "coming on strong was not a bad idea," since "you get no attention by being nice."[53]

A major policy area where the Human Rights Bureau under Derian "came on strong" and thus triggered opposition from regional bureaus was the implementation of Section 502B of the amended Foreign Assistance Act. Under this legislative mandate, that security assistance was to be contingent on human rights considerations, the bureau took a number of steps that constituted a direct challenge to the regional bureaus, who saw security assistance as one of the major tools they could use in their dealings with the countries in their geographic areas.

One of the points on which the bureau attacked the position of the regional bureaus was the latters' belief that human rights could be either bypassed or given no more consideration than any of a number of other policy factors. The bureau took the opposite view, insisting that the human rights conditions in Section 502B had to be met before security aid could be given. A second point of bureau attack on the policy primacy claimed by the regional bureaus concerned the informational basis on which policy decisions were made. Refusing to accept the career bureaucracy's reports as the final word on the status of human rights in countries to which U.S. aid might be extended, the bureau created its own information channels and thus put itself in position to argue the question of eligibility for aid on a factual basis. Finally, the bureau questioned the arguments of those who sought to justify aid to countries with poor human records on the ground that this country's security interests made this assistance necessary.[54]

The Human Rights Bureau's aggressive discharge of its legislative mandate was thus one of the factors creating the bureaucratic struggle that went on around the Carter administration's human rights policy. As a party to this conflict, however, the bureau suffered from a number of handicaps, not the least of which was a level of funding and staffing that some have described as "limited" and others as "inadequate." Not everyone, however, shared this feeling concerning the adequacy of the bureau's personnel resources. Warren Christopher, for example, testified to a congressional subcommittee that the bureau "has specialists in security and development assistance as well as officers working on international organization affairs and on liaison with non-governmental organizations." Moreover, continued Christopher, the work of the Bureau was aided and implemented by the presence in each U.S. embassy and each geographical bureau of an officer with primary human rights responsibility.

Opinion was thus divided on the question of the adequacy of the personnel of the Human Rights Bureau. One reason for doubts concerning the bureau's human resources was a rather pervasive feeling that it would not be able to attract the strong, capable people it needed to compete successfully in the bureaucratic struggle. This feeling stemmed from a belief that service in the Human Rights Bureau would ruin an individual's career prospects. One of Derian's tasks as she assumed office was therefore to try to change this perception. "Human Rights," she asserted, "is not a penal colony, or a way station." She took this problem to Secretary Vance, seeking assurance that the people assigned to Human Rights would go on from there to good positions. As she later observed, "this did happen"; only one Human Rights staff member "got stuck, and blamed this on his Human Rights service; but this was unfounded: only an excuse."[55]

As a participant in the bureaucratic conflict over the direction of U.S. foreign policy, the Human Rights Bureau had to deal with other problems, for example, being included in the decision-making process. When this point was raised during one congressional hearing, Derian admitted that there were times when she felt that she was being left out of this process. When this happened, "I assert myself."[56]

Another problem with which the bureau had to contend was access to all the information that was relevant to its work and that would enable it to deal effectively with policy questions. Thus, in the same hearing Derian commented that "all the cables I would like to see don't always come." It was also her feeling, however, that she "didn't miss much," because if her office was missed on the regular distribution of information, someone would notice the omission and tell her what cables she should ask for.[57]

Not all observers of the bureaucratic scene were convinced that Human Rights had all the information it needed. One such observer was "concerned about the adequacy of the support from the Bureau of Intelligence and Research for human rights matters," and another believed:

[The human rights people] suffer some of the difficulties we do, of not having access to information that the desk people do have. . . . There are some internal communications problems within the State Department that make the work of the Human Rights Bureau less effective than it might be if there were full cooperation.[58]

The focal point for the policy conflicts involving the Human Rights Bureau and other agencies was the "Christopher Group." This was the name given to the Interagency Group on Human Rights and Foreign Assistance established by a National Security Council directive of April 1, 1977. It met for the first time the following month with representatives of all interested State Department bureaus and offices and from the Treasury, Defense, Agriculture, Commerce, and Labor departments and the National Security Council and the Export-Import Bank. The group was chaired by Deputy Secretary of State Warren Christopher; hence its name. Although it did not deal with the full range of human rights policy, the Christopher Group was a highly significant factor in the formulation and implementation of the Carter administration's human rights policy. The group's importance grew from its concern with the most sensitive aspect of this policy: foreign assistance. In dealing with this subject, it was assisted by a working group composed of deputies and assistants from the agencies represented and co-chaired by the two agencies that took opposing views on the extent to which human rights considerations should control assistance programs: the Human Rights Bureau and the Bureau of Economic and Business Affairs.

Originally seen as a means of arriving at a unified position to take to its parent body, the working group proved unable to resolve the disagreements among its members. Consequently it became an arena of debate within which the various agencies presented the arguments that would later be heard in the Christopher Group, and what thus came out of this process was a definition of areas of agreement and disagreement on specific aid proposals.

The process by which the Christopher Group dealt with these points of controversy was essentially litigation: an adversarial, confrontational procedure in which the various disputants presented their case through action memorandums and oral arguments. As Patricia Derian described it, the outcome of all this debate "depended on whether your paper was compelling enough . . . and whether you were really hot that day and could be eloquent enough."[59]

The Christopher Group's first function was to provide an opportunity for all interested parties to present all points of view on particular assistance problems. The next step was to attempt to find a middle ground, or compromise, between those who wanted assistance denied to countries guilty of human rights violations and those who contended that such refusal would do serious damage to other important U.S. interests.[60]

Carter's deputy secretary of state, Warren Christopher, was a central figure in this search for a middle ground between competing policy demands, as he was also in relation to decision making in specific cases. The precise form of this process depended on the situation at hand. Thus, when asked who made the decision about granting aid to a particular country, when there was a split among the groups involved in the policy discussions, Christopher's reply was that it depended on the type of aid. If, for example, the issue was a U.S. vote in a multilateral development bank and there was a split in the Interagency Committee, he would consider the question and "frequently" discuss it with Secretary Vance. From this discussion a recommendation would go to the treasury secretary, who actually directed this vote. Other cases exhibited a similar pattern of interagency discussion, consultation between Christopher and Vance, and then decision, with Christopher being the ultimate decider.[61]

This process for handling conflict over the human rights issue was the subject of some adverse criticism. One comment charged that the high level of policy conflict "was compounded by Christopher's preference for flexible policy and disinclination to exercise decisive personal leadership. . . . [He was] reluctant to openly commit himself to a particular course of action in the name of his client, the Secretary of State." Some members of the Christopher Group saw its discussion process as a "sterile exchange" of predictable arguments by the Human Rights Bureau and the regional bureaus. These agencies, according to these critics, came to meetings with only one purpose: to defend, not change, their positions.[62]

Others, however, saw the policy-making process in a more favorable light. Thus, some members of the Christopher Group asserted that the group's procedures offered a "valuable bureaucratic experience." In their opinion, the function of a bureaucracy is "to bring the best possible information and analysis to those responsible for making decisions. Actors can make their best presentations, as they did in the Christopher Group." The group's efforts were also commended for being successful in achieving one of its goals: exposing each element in the human rights bureaucracy to the viewpoints of others.[63]

At stake in all this was the fate of the human rights concern that Jimmy Carter had declared to be a central focus of his administration's foreign policy. Despite this clear commitment, backed by and supporting legislation with the same intent, the Human Rights Bureau under Patricia Derian was by no means a consistent winner in the policy battles. Speaking to this point, she observed, "I'm not there as an accountant: I'm there to make changes and uphold the law." She was satisfied, however, that she had done a lot better than she or anyone else had expected. "I think my average is better than it would seem to be. . . . I'm doing OK, or I would have gone."[64]

As far as policy substance was concerned, the Carter administration's procedures, particularly those of the Christopher Group, have been criticized because of their emphasis on the case-by-case approach. This approach was the result of a deliberate strategy choice that involved rejection of the alternative: the development of a general, long-term human rights policy, with clearly defined principles on which to base decisions in specific cases. This alternative was turned down partly because many specific decisions would have had to be delayed while the overall policy was being hammered out, but mainly because of the preference, notably by Christopher, for the inductive, case-by-case tactic.[65]

In one sense, then, the Carter administration's human rights policy was a series of case-by-case decisions reached through the bureaucratic conflict process, a fact that led some to charge that the policy lacked consistency. However, as Stanley J. Heginbotham pointed out, in time, "a significant measure of consensus had begun to emerge among working level officials as to certain generalizations that seemed to shape the making of human rights decisions." His report then listed the generalizations, which provided the basis from which one could develop a "plausible interpretation of U.S. human rights initiatives that shows a significant measure of policy coherence." They are:

1. Severe violations of integrity of the person should receive high priority in U.S. policy concerns.

2. Levels of human rights performance can be expected to differ from country to country.

3. Human rights initiatives should be suspended or curtailed when they threaten other significant U.S. interests.

4. The leverage available to the United States with respect to specific countries should be a significant factor in determining the amount of human rights attention they receive.

5. Human rights initiatives will be responsive to incremental changes in levels of violations as well as to absolute levels.

6. Though public pressures and direct leverage can be effective instruments of human rights policy, quiet diplomatic efforts and indirect hints of linkage between human rights conditions and U.S. support are often likely to be more successful.

7. In determining the appropriateness of different instruments of human rights policy purposes, consideration should be given to the direct effect an action would have on human rights conditions in a country, to the likely cost of an action to U.S. interests, and to the amount of leverage an action affords the United States.[66]

The intense bureaucratic conflict that characterized the effort to give effect to the Carter administration's commitment to human rights thus led eventually to a list of generalizations that could be said to represent this administration's human rights policy. This conflict became less bitter as the administration's tenure in office progressed, because of several factors. First, the administration's views on how the balance between human rights and other interests was to be struck became more evident; second, precedents tended to diminish the areas of conflict; and third, members of the bureaucracy became accustomed to considering human rights when policy decisions were being made.[67]

The Reagan Administration

The part played by the bureaucracy under the Reagan administration in determining whether or not U.S. foreign policy would express a strong human rights concern differed markedly from its role during Carter's term in office. In the Carter era, the bureaucracy's task was to resolve the conflict between an aggressive Human Rights Bureau, on the one hand, and on the other, regional bureaus whose interests and traditional practices led them to resist the injection of human rights into the foreign policy-making process. When Ronald Reagan assumed office, however, he faced an entirely different situation since the bureaucratic struggle that characterized so much of the previous administration's life had virtually disappeared.

The relative absence of conflict over human rights policy in the Reagan administration has been attributed to a number of factors, one being the nature and performance of the Human Rights Bureau. This office, according to one viewpoint, did not function as a vigorous promoter of human rights whose actions would precipitate conflict over the substance and direction of foreign policy, principally because the administration never intended the bureau to be a forceful advocate. The early performance of the Reagan administration certainly provided little reason for anyone to believe that it wanted an aggressive bureau. Thus, according to Reagan's first secretary of state, Alexander Haig, there was no need for a human rights bureau "because we're all concerned with human rights."[68] And when Reagan was making his appointments to various offices, he chose for his assistant secretary of state for human rights and humanitarian affairs Ernest W. Lefever, who had emphatically denounced Carter's human rights policy and termed human rights "a confusing guideline for responsible statecraft." This nomination was seen as evidence that the Reagan administration was hostile to human rights, an impression that was strengthened by the president's refusal for months to submit another candidate for the post after the Senate Foreign Relations Committee rejected the Lefever nomination.[69]

The Human Rights Bureau was thus allowed to limp along for almost a year with only interim leadership. Moreover, because of the prevailing perception of Reagan's attitude toward human rights and the way the administration was treating the bureau, this office was not seen as a desirable posting and hence was not able to attract high-quality personnel. The net effect of all this was a Human Rights Bureau that in the early stages of the administration was "easily overridden" in the interagency debates over foreign policy.[70]

Even the appointment in late 1981 of Elliott Abrams, respected as a competent administrator, to head the Human Rights Bureau did not, in the opinion of some observers, make the bureau a positive, effective force for human rights. Writing in 1984, for example, Caleb Rossiter concluded that, although it had been revitalized and restaffed, the bureau "was not the contentious, staunch advocate of human rights that it was under Derian or even the more cooperative but still dedicated advocate it was under the acting Bureau head, Stephen Palmer." The bureau, Rossiter asserted,

was relegated to a low, uncontroversial status. Operating more as a public relations bureau for anti-Communism, the Bureau rarely threatens the interests and domain of the geographic bureaus or the security agencies, and so no longer engenders the conflicts it did under Derian.[71]

The Reagan administration's Human Rights Bureau has thus been seen as a much less formidable, positive force for human rights than it had been under Carter, playing a less active role because of the "restricted objectives of [the administration's] human rights policy" and in general the "minor place given to human rights in the Reagan foreign policy." Given this situation, as one former bureau staff member observed, "there were very few instances when the Bureau felt impelled to press for action; and unless this office takes this leadership in the interests of human rights, there is no policy conflict within the bureaucracy."[72]

Other critics of the Human Rights Bureau as it functioned under Reagan have described it as "weak," "weak-kneed," "weaker under Abrams than under Derian," "not advancing the cause of human rights in most areas," "lacking adequate contact with other sectors of the State Department," and operating under procedures in which "there . . . is no meaningful consultation; only memoranda." The bureau has also been accused of failing to develop a meaningful human rights policy, of lacking an independent agenda, and of tending to distort and politicize the substance of human rights. Finally, the charge has been made that "when the Reagan Administration's policies conflict with the promotion of human rights, Secretary Abrams endorsed and explained those policies rather than exercising his [legal] mandate of advocating human rights concerns both publicly and within the State Department's bureaucracy."[73]

All in all, it is clear that the Reagan administration's Human Rights Bureau has been perceived as having little ability to influence foreign policy decisions to make them expressive of a human rights concern. This situation, in turn, is seen as being the product of two factors: (1) a negative attitude toward human rights on the part of the administration, and (2) the failure of the bureau and its head to act as an agency charged through legislation with the responsibility for pressing the claims of human rights whenever foreign policy decisions are being made.

There is, however, another and more favorable perception of the character and significance of the Reagan administration's Human Rights Bureau, its commitment to promoting human rights within the bureaucracy, and its ability to do this effectively. As far as the bureau itself is concerned, the responsibilities to be discharged were the same as those under the Carter administration:

1. To monitor the human rights situation in every country.

2. To propose policy actions concerning all countries.

3. To initiate instructions to embassies.

4. To pose questions to embassies for investigation.

5. To maintain liaison with geographic bureaus and the embassies of their countries in Washington.[74]

While the Human Rights Bureau thus retained, at least formally, the basic functions it had under Carter, it continued the evolutionary process that saw it grow from its very small dimensions at the time Patricia Derian came to office to its 1985 staff of fifty people supervising an expanded scope of operations. Qualitatively, the bureau has been described as "having excellent career people and good morale, a more comfortable place for career people, with less bureaucratic confrontation; the dialogue between the bureau and others is now more collegial than it was previously." The bureau's importance in the State Department was seen as having been enhanced because of the personal prominence of its head through much of Reagan's tenure in office, Elliott Abrams, a factor that has probably enhanced the bureau's ability to gain the cooperation of other sectors of the bureaucracy. Abrams himself was able to convince at least some observers that he was truly committed to human rights.[75]

A bright picture has thus been painted of a Human Rights Bureau that was able to attract the "intelligent, aggressive" people it said it wanted, people who came to this office feeling that service there would be good for their careers, and a bureau that could function with less conflict than it had during the Carter administration. If, indeed, this picture is accurate, then it is obvious that the Reagan bureau was reaping the fruits of the intense and often frustrating struggle by its predecessor to win a place for human rights within the bureaucracy. The battle within the bureaucracy to establish the legitimacy of human rights, in other words, had been fought and won. As a result of this struggle and with the passage of time the regional bureaus had become more willing to accept the role of the Human Rights Bureau in the policy process and less inclined to see its activities as an invasion of their domain and an injection of an irritant—human rights—into their dealings with other governments.[76]

The conclusion to be drawn from this experience, as one State Department official expressed it, is that "human rights is here to stay." Those who agree support their belief by pointing to what they see as evidence that the Reagan administration's Human Rights Bureau did indeed play a positive part in the formulation and implementation of foreign policy. This "evidence" consists of such bureau actions as sending cables to ambassadors who, in its opinion, were not being as active and effective as they should in presenting this country's concern over certain human rights situations; raising objections that prevented Chile's eligibility certification for U.S. assistance; resisting proposals to export cattle prods to South Africa on the ground that these instruments would be used for repressive purposes; taking a policy initiative in respect to the human rights situation in Indonesia; exercising clearance and preparing instructions on items appearing on the agenda of the UN's Commission on Human Rights; and examining security assistance at all levels of the decision-making process to be sure that human rights was entered into the equation.[77]

POLITICAL SOURCES OF HUMAN RIGHTS POLICIES: CONGRESS

Despite the tendency of administrations generally to resist efforts of Congress to play a significant role in making this country's foreign policy, Congress was, in fact, an influential factor in the formulation and implementation of the human rights policies of the Carter and Reagan administrations. The most obvious and direct form of this policy impact has been noted in connection with the legislative basis of human rights policy. Congress has also contributed substantially to the policies of these two administrations by holding hearings on human rights-related issues.

Congressional hearings have been an important part of the policy formation process for a number of reasons. By evaluating human rights situations in particular countries, these proceedings provide information that the human rights bureaucracy can use in determining where and what kind of human rights action to take. The realization that Congress possesses this information can also serve as a spur to administrative action. Again, hearings supply a check on the adequacy of the annual country reports and other sources of information available to policy makers. Finally, hearings involving inquiries into the effectiveness of current human rights policies and programs can stimulate efforts to improve them.[78]

Through hearings, direct representations, and other methods, Congress can provide evidence that it is monitoring the implementation of human rights policy: by looking for improper use of loopholes in human rights laws, noting inconsistent behavior by various agencies, expressing concern over specific policy decisions, and asking for explanations of certain decisions.[79] Congress's human rights policy role involves exerting pressure on the administration to act, as well as the monitoring of its performance. It can, for example, press for greater use of the leverage, in the form of sanctions, provided in human rights laws. The effectiveness of such congressional efforts to move an administration to act depends on a number of factors, including how resistant the administration is in general to congressional foreign policy initiatives and how committed the administration and the foreign policy bureaucracy are to human rights. In the absence of a strong commitment Congress has an important part to play: providing support for those elements in the administration and the bureaucracy that want to see human rights occupy a prominent place in U.S. foreign policy. This support, for example, can be most useful to U.S. diplomats as they confront leaders of other governments on human rights issues, because the diplomats can cite congressional concern as a basis for what they are doing.[80]

The Carter Administration

In the eyes of some of its critics, the Carter administration seemed to be demonstrating the typical Executive Branch tendency to resist congressional foreign policy initiatives, even when those initiatives involved the policy area to which the administration had made such a strong official commitment. President Carter, for example, was accused of "consistently opposing Congressional efforts to tighten existing laws prohibiting military and economic aid to governments cited for 'gross and consistent' violations of human rights."[81]

To the standard contention by administrations that legislation in the foreign policy field would tie their hands and deprive them of the flexibility needed for the effective conduct of foreign affairs, the Carter administration added some specific objections to proposed congressional action. Thus, it opposed a proposed trade embargo against the repressive Ugandan regime of Idi Amin on the grounds that such action would violate the principle of free trade to which this country was committed. Again, when asked whether Congress should make loans by American commercial banks conditional on human rights considerations, Carter said no, adding that any such restriction "would violate the principles of our own free enterprise system."[82]

Several considerations could serve to place the Carter administration's attitude toward congressional initiatives in a more positive light. Opposition to new human rights legislation, for example, could have stemmed from the administration's belief, as expressed by one Human Rights Bureau official, that "we have enough law to do what we want to do."[83] Furthermore, the fact that the administration opposed some new legislation did not rule out the possibility that it would welcome other forms of congressional participation in the process of developing a human rights policy. This, at least, is a conclusion that could be drawn from Warren Christopher's statement to a congressional subcommittee during a discussion of aid to Paraguay.

We pay a great deal of attention to the views of the people on Capitol Hill. If you were to indicate that you thought this particular decision was an unwise one, it would influence our future decisions. . . . I would always welcome an opportunity to talk with you on these individual decisions, to see if we couldn't reach common ground.[84]

At the same time, Christopher offered to provide the appropriate congressional subcommittee with the agenda for Interagency Committees meetings. If the congressional group wanted to have some input when these meetings were held, "we would be glad to receive it."[85]

Whether welcomed by the Carter administration or not, Congress did take a number of actions designed to insure that human rights had a significant place in the making of foreign policy. Thus, Congressman Don Bonker, chairman of the Subcommittee on International Organizations, wrote on the committee's behalf to President Carter before Carter visited South Korea, asking the president to speak out publicly concerning the human rights situation there. Representative Bonker was also one of a group of congressmen who wrote to the secretary of state "strongly urging" a change in the

U.S. policy of supporting a seat for the Kampuchean Pol Pot regime, condemned for its human rights abuses, in the UN General Assembly.[86]

Congress occasionally enjoyed some success in these efforts to influence Carter's human rights policy. Congressional pressure was credited with responsibility for the trade embargo Carter eventually imposed on Uganda, which probably contributed to the downfall of the oppressive Idi Amin regime. Again, Congressional insistence led to a more confrontational U.S. report on Soviet performance under the human rights provisions of the Helsinki Declaration than would otherwise have been produced. Finally, a change in U.S. aid to the Philippines, from military to economic, was attributed to a recommendation from a congressional subcommittee.[87]

In addition to these cases there are other indications that Congress did have some impact on the Carter administration's human rights policy. Stephen Cohen, for example, concluded that the possibility that Congress would adopt country-specific human rights legislation "appeared to have had significant influence on the . . . administration," and the "threat to the passage of the foreign assistance bill coming from Congressman Charles Wilson" was said to have affected the administration's behavior in regard to the human rights situation in Nicaragua.[88]

Finally, Congress influenced the formulation and implementation of the Carter administration's human rights policy by lending support for what the administration was trying to do. National Security Advisor Zbigniew Brzezinski, for example, has noted that the council's initiative to reduce U.S. arms sales to countries guilty of serious human rights abuses "met with a positive response from Capitol Hill," and Donald Fraser pointed to the part congressional groups could play in "helping to maintain the momentum of this administration by observing the intramural disputes within the Executive Branch and lending appropriate support to those forces which are committed to a strong human rights policy." Patricia Derian testified to the reality of this support when she quoted the remark one under secretary of state made to her: "Look, we can't do anything with you. We know you've got the whole Hill with you."[89]

The Reagan Administration

If comments by Secretary of State Shultz can be taken as expressing the Reagan administration's feelings on the subject, this administration's attitude toward the relationship of Congress to human rights policy fell in the same "yes-but" category that tends to characterize administrations in general on the subject of Congress and foreign policy. In remarks that presumably reflected the thinking of the administration of which he was a part, Secretary Shultz observed:

there is no doubt that Congressional concerns and pressures have played a positive role in giving impetus and backing to our efforts to influence other governments' behavior. This Congressional pressure can strengthen the hand of the executive in its efforts of diplomacy. At the same time, there can be complications if the legislative instrument is too inflexible or heavy-handed or, even more, if Congress attempts to take on the administrative responsibility for executing policy.

Assistant Secretary of State Elliott Abrams also expressed mixed feelings on the subject when he assured a congressional subcommittee that he looked forward to working with them, but also voiced his concern that members of Congress were inclined to pay too much attention to "narrow questions" in their discussion of human rights policy.[90]

For its part, Congress was evidently quite determined to have some say concerning the formulation and implementation of the Reagan administration's human rights policy. Actions in pursuing this objective included two House resolutions, one urging the president to suspend aid to Liberia until it improved its human rights record and made progress toward democracy, and another registering support for a National Accord produced by Chilean political leaders, calling for a peaceful return to democracy in that country. This latter action was accompanied by a statement by the resolutions's author, Congressman Michael D. Barnes, expressing the hope that President Reagan would "embrace the [Chilean] initiative."

Members of Congress also saw hearings as opportunities to tell members of the Reagan administration what they thought should be done about certain human rights issues. On one such occasion Elliott Abrams was asked to convey to Secretary Shultz a representative's opinion that the delay in granting the request by a Chinese woman's tennis champion to stay in the United States was a violation of human rights. During the same hearing, one congressman expressed his and his colleagues' hope that the administration would grant asylum in the United States to victims of Iran's persecution of Baha'is, while another House member asked the State Department to investigate the treatment of members of the black Hebrew community in Israel more carefully.

Illustrative of another technique for influencing the administration's human rights policy was the letter to Treasury Secretary Donald Regan by forty-nine congressmen protesting the administration's decision to support multilateral bank loans to Chile, Argentina, Paraguay, Uruguay, and South Korea. Congress also occasionally expressed support for what the administration was doing as, for example, in relation to the question of human rights in Romania.[91]

While Congress's capacity to have an impact on an administration's human rights policy is very difficult to determine, it appears that the legislative branch did exert some influence on the Reagan administration. Thus, according to an October 1981 confidential memo to the secretary of state, a fundamental policy shift toward including human rights in the administration's agenda became necessary because "the Congressional belief that we have no consistent human rights policy threatens to disrupt important foreign policy initiatives." Again, the watchdog function of Congress has been seen as a "principal component" in the administration's policy vis-à-vis El Salvador and other Central American countries.[92]

SUMMARY

Both similarities and differences are discernible between the Carter and Reagan administrations on the point of the influence on their human rights policies of international agreements and national laws. While both administrations professed to base their policies on international human rights agreements, reference to this policy base was more prominent and explicit in the Carter administration than in its successor. The impression that international human rights treaties held a higher place in the thinking of the Carter administration than in that of Reagan is strengthened by the fact that gaining U.S. adherence to these instruments appeared to be a matter of greater concern to the Carter than to the Reagan administration.

Both administrations functioned under a set of national laws that mandated the injection of human rights considerations into foreign policy decision making, particularly when this process involved the question of U.S. military, security, and economic assistance to other countries. Both administrations were accused of circumventing or ignoring these laws and thereby failing to execute them faithfully. Any conclusion as to the validity of this charge must take into account the fact that human rights laws contain qualifications ("loopholes") that open the door to the exercise of executive discretion, and both administrations took advantage of this opening as occasion seemed to demand. Whether or not this opportunity was abused and human rights thus unjustifiably sacrificed on the altars of "basic human needs" and/or "vital security interests" is a question whose answer turns on one's view of how the balance is to be struck between human rights and other foreign policy considerations. Any attempt to differentiate between the two administrations at the point of greater or lesser tendency to look for ways to get around national human rights laws runs into one frustrating variable: the nature of the international and national political environment prevailing at the time when foreign policy decisions must be made. This is an important factor, since it affects judgments concerning the relative weight that is to be given to the various interests that must be considered in making decisions.

Among the political factors affecting the formulation and implementation of these policies, a distinct difference is found in their experience with the bureaucracy. Whereas most of Carter's tenure in office was marked by intense bureaucratic conflict over the inclusion of human rights in foreign policy considerations, this struggle had virtually ended by the time Reagan assumed the presidency, and human rights had come to be accepted as a legitimate foreign policy element. The role of the bureaucracy thus changed from that of limiting the administration's ability to make U.S. foreign policy express a human rights concern as it did under Carter, to that of substantially supporting such emphasis as the administration chose to give to human rights as it did under Reagan.

The role of the other political source of influence, Congress, was the same for both administrations in several respects. One similarity was the determination on the part of Congress to be both an initiator and a monitor of human rights policy. A second common note was evidence in the records of the two administrations that Congress enjoyed some success in influencing policy. The two experiences were also alike in that both administrations gave indications that, like all administrations, they had limited enthusiasm for a prominent congressional role in matters related to foreign affairs, including human rights.

While the role of Congress in the two administrations thus had a number of similarities, there was one difference: the impact of Congress on the Reagan administration's human rights policy was in the direction of inducing a policy change, in contrast to the essentially supportive influence that Congress exerted on the Carter administration. This difference stems from the fact that, while the Carter administration came into office with a clear commitment to the human rights foreign policy focus that characterized numerous laws enacted by Congress, the Reagan administration's first actions were seen as antithetical to the purpose of this legislation.

NOTES

1. U.S. Congress, House of Representatives, Committee on Foreign Affairs, *Human Rights Documents: Compilation of Documents Pertaining to Human Rights* (Washington, D.C.: U.S. Government Printing Office, 1983), p. 28.

2. U.S. Congress, House of Representatives, Committee on Foreign Affairs, *Human Rights and U.S. Foreign Policy: Hearings Before the Subcommittee on International Organizations*, 96th Cong., 1st Sess., May 2 and 10; June 21; July 12; and August 2, 1979, p. 235.

3. *Filartiga* v. *Pena*, 676 F. 2d 876, 884 (2d Cir. 1980), cited in Cynthia Brown, ed., *With Friends Like These*, The Americas Watch Report on Human Rights and U.S. Policy in Latin America (New York: Pantheon Books, 1985), p. 27.

4. Stephen B. Cohen, "Conditioning U.S. Security Assistance on Human Rights Practices," *American Journal of International Law* 76 (January-April 1982): 246.

5. This assertion was made in a statement by the American League for Exports and Security Assistance, in U.S. Congress, *Human Rights and U.S. Foreign Policy*, p. 452.

6. Patricia Derian quoted in Vassily Aksynov, "Overhaul U.S. Human Rights Policy?" *U.S. News and World Report*, March 2, 1981, p. 49.

7. Zbigniew Brzezinski, *Power and Principle*, rev. ed. (New York: Farrar, Straus, and Giroux, 1985), p. 55.

8. U.S. Congress, *Human Rights and U.S. Foreign Policy*, p. 38.

9. Richard Lillich, in U.S. Congress, House of Representatives, Committee on

Foreign Affairs, *Political Killings by Governments of Their Citizens: Hearings before the Subcommittee on Human Rights and International Organizations*, 98th Cong., 1st Sess., November 16 and 17, 1983 (Washington D.C.: U.S. Government Printing Office, 1983), p. 76, and U.S. Congress, *Human Rights and U.S. Foreign Policy*, p. 70.

10. This perspective on the proposed reservations follows conversations with personnel of the Department of State and Justice Department.

11. James Thyden, Department of State Official, address in Chicago, October 26, 1984.

12. David Carliner, in U.S. Congress, House of Representatives, Committee on Foreign Affairs, *Review of U.S. Human Rights Policy: Hearings before the Subcommittee on Human Rights and International Organizations*, 98th Cong., 1st Sess., March 3; June 28; and September 21, 1983 (Washington, D.C.: U.S. Government Printing Office, 1983), p. 48.

13. Americas Watch, Helsinki Watch, Lawyers Committee for International Human Rights, *The Reagan Administration's Human Rights Policy: A Mid-Term Review* (New York and Washington, D.C.: Author, 1982), pp. 10–11 (Hereafter cited as *Mid-Term Review*).

14. Conversation with the author at the Department of State, September 1985.

15. Lawyers Committee for Human Rights and The Watch Committees, *The Reagan Administration's Record on Human Rights in 1985* (New York and Washington D.C.: Author, 1986), p. 21.

16. Michael Posner, in U.S. Congress, *Political Killings*, p. 180.

17. Robin Toner, "After 37 Years, Senate Endorses a Genocide Ban," *The New York Times*, February 20, 1986.

18. U.S. Congress, House of Representatives, Committee on Foreign Affairs, *The Phenomenon of Torture: Hearings and Markup before the Committee on Foreign Affairs and the Subcommittee*, 98th Cong., 2d Sess., May 15 and 16 and September 6, 1984 (Washington, D.C.: U.S. Government Printing Office, 1984), p. 169.

19. For the background and development of human rights legislation, see Brown, *With Friends Like These*, pp. 30–32; David Heaps, *Human Rights and U.S. Foreign Policy: The First Decade, 1973–1983* (New York: American Association for the International Commission of Jurists, 1984), pp. 9–14; U.S. Congress, *Human Rights and U.S. Foreign Policy*, pp. 299–300 and 343–344; Cohen, "Conditioning U.S. Security Assistance," pp. 249–350; and U.S. Congress, House of Representatives, Committee on Foreign Affairs, *Human Rights Documents: Compilation of Documents Pertaining to Human Rights* (Washington, D.C.: U.S. Government Printing Office, 1983), pp. 24–29.

20. Cohen, "Conditioning U.S. Security Assistance," p. 246.

21. U.S. Congress, *Human Rights and U.S. Foreign Policy*, p. 305.

22. Patricia Derian, conversation with the author, September 1985, and Warren Christopher, in U.S. Congress, *Human Rights and U.S. Foreign Policy*, p. 21.

23. Cohen, "Conditioning U.S. Security Assistance," p. 264.

24. Jo Marie Greisgraber, in U.S. Congress, *Human Rights and U.S. Foreign Policy*, p. 155.

25. Jim Morrell, *Achievement of the 1970s: U.S. Human Rights Law and Policy*, International Policy Report (Washington, D.C.: Center for International Policy, 1981), p. 3.

26. U.S. Congress, *Human Rights and U.S. Foreign Policy*, p. 252.

27. Greisgraber, in U.S. Congress, *Human Rights and U.S. Foreign Policy*, p. 156.

28. David Weissbrodt, in U.S. Congress, *Human Rights and U.S. Foreign Policy*, pp. 162–163 and 165.

29. Cohen, "Conditioning U.S. Security Assistance," p. 276.

30. Warren Christopher, in U.S. Congress, *Human Rights and U.S. Foreign Policy*, p. 36, and Stephen B. Cohen, in U.S. Congress, *Review of U.S. Human Rights Policy*, p. 180.

31. *Mid-Term Review*, p. 6.

32. Americas Watch, Helsinki Watch, Lawyers Committee for International Human Rights, *Failure: The Reagan Administration's Human Rights Policy in 1983* (New York and Washington, D.C.: Author, 1984), p. 6 (Hereafter cited as *Failure*).

33. Lawyers Committee for Human Rights, *The Reagan Administration's Record*, p. 8.

34. The cases cited are referred to in *Mid-Term Review*, pp. 7–8; U.S. Congress, *Review of U.S. Human Rights Policy*, p. 43; *Failure*, pp. 48, 69; and Lawyers Committee for Human Rights, *The Reagan Administration's Record*, p. 14.

35. Americas Watch, Helsinki Watch, Lawyers Committee for International Human Rights, *In the Face of Cruelty: The Reagan Administration's Human Rights Record in 1984* (New York and Washington, D.C.: Author, 1985), p. 42 (Hereafter cited as *In the Face of Cruelty*).

36. David B. Ottoway, "Embargo on Ethiopia Ruled Out," *The Washington Post*, September 11, 1985.

37. U.S. Congress, *Review of U.S. Human Rights Policy*, pp. 150–151.

38. U.S. Congress, *The Phenomenon of Torture*, pp. 167–168.

39. Ibid., p. 172.

40. *Failure*, pp. 37–38.

41. Morton H. Halperin and Arnold Kanter, *Readings in American Foreign Policy: A Bureaucratic Perspective* (Boston: Little, Brown, 1973), p. 10, quoted in Marian Irish and Elke Frank, eds., *U.S. Foreign Policy: Context, Conduct, and Content* (New York: Harcourt, Brace, Jovanovich, 1975), p. 331.

42. Cohen, "Conditioning U.S. Security Assistance," p. 257.

43. C. Clyde Ferguson, in U.S. Congress, *Review of U.S. Human Rights Policy*, p. 156.

44. Brian Atwood, *Plain Talk on Human Rights*, Current Issues (Washington, D.C.: Center for International Policy, 1981), p. 5.

45. Stanley J. Heginbotham, in U.S. Congress, *Human Rights and U.S. Foreign Policy*, p. 114.

46. For the forms and sources of resistance to Carter's human rights policy, see Cohen, "Conditioning U.S. Security Assistance," pp. 259–260, and Caleb Rossiter, *Human Rights: The Carter Record, the Reagan Reaction*, International Policy Report (Washington, D.C.: Center for International Policy, 1984), p. 4 (hereafter cited as *Carter Record, Reagan Reaction*).

47. Conversations at the Department of State in 1984 and 1985; Cohen, "Conditioning U.S. Security Assistance," pp. 249, 256–257; and *Carter Record, Reagan Reaction*, pp. 1, 4.

48. *Carter Record, Reagan Reaction*, p. 5.

49. Conversations at the Department of State, October 1984, and *Carter Record, Reagan Reaction*, pp. 4–5.

50. Cohen, "Conditioning U.S. Security Assistance," p. 261.

51. Conversation with Patricia Derian, September 1985.

52. Ibid.

53. Conversations at the Department of State, October 1984, and May and September 1985.

54. Cohen, "Conditioning U.S. Security Assistance," p. 261.

55. U.S. Congress, *Human Rights and U.S. Foreign Policy*, pp. 333, 361, 382, 390, 404; U.S. Congress, House of Representatives, Committee on Foreign Affairs, *Human Rights in Asia: Non-Communist Countries: Hearings before the Subcommittees on Asian and Pacific Affairs and International Organizations* 96th Cong., 2d Sess., February 4, 6 and 7, 1980 (Washington, D.C.: U.S. Government Printing Office, 1980), p. 278; *Human Rights: The First Decade*, p. 23; and conversation with Patricia Derian, September 1985. During the Carter administration the bureau increased in size to twenty persons, including three deputy assistant secretaries and twelve human rights officers. Cohen, "Conditioning U.S. Security Assistance," note 79.

56. U.S. Congress, *Human Rights in Asia: Non-Communist Countries*, p. 178. In Derian's opinion, some of the failure to include the Human Rights office in decision making was "inadvertent."

57. Ibid., p. 178.

58. Pharis J. Harvey, in Ibid., p. 149, and Heginbotham, in U.S. Congress, *Human Rights and U.S. Foreign Policy*, p. 361.

59. Atwood, *Plain Talk on Human Rights*, p. 3.

60. U.S. Congress, *Human Rights and U.S. Foreign Policy*, p. 345.

61. Ibid., pp. 33–35.

62. *Carter Record, Reagan Reaction*, pp. 4, 20.

63. Ibid., p. 62.

64. U.S. Congress, House of Representatives, Committee on Foreign Affairs, *Human Rights in Asia: Communist Countries: Hearing before the Subcommittees on Asian and Pacific Affairs and International Organizations*, October 1, 1980 (Washington, D.C.: U.S. Government Printing Office, 1980), p. 52; U.S. Congress, *Review of U.S. Human Rights Policy*, p. 157; and conversation with Patricia Derian, September 1985.

65. *Carter Record, Reagan Reaction*, p. 6.

66. U.S. Congress, *Human Rights and U.S. Foreign Policy*, pp. 347–350.

67. Conversations at the Department of State, May and September 1985.

68. U.S. Congress, *Review of U.S. Human Rights Policy*, p. 38.

69. *Carter Record, Reagan Reaction*, p. 22.

70. Ibid., pp. 22–23, and conversations at the Department of State, October 1984.

71. *Carter Record, Reagan Reaction*, pp. 22, 25.

72. Ibid., p. 25, and conversations at the Department of State, May 1985.

73. Conversations with former Human Rights Bureau personnel; *Human Rights: The First Decade*, p. 43; *Failure*, p. 16; *In the Face of Cruelty*, p. 108; and Brown, *With Friends Like These*, pp. 8, 11.

74. Conversations at the Department of State, October 1984.

75. Ibid., and *Failure*, p. 19.

76. Conversations at the Department of State, October 1984.

77. Ibid.

78. U.S. Congress, *Human Rights and U.S. Foreign Policy*, p. 167, and U.S. Congress, *Human Rights in Asia: Non-Communist Countries*, p. 1.

79. U.S. Congress, *Human Rights and U.S. Foreign Policy*, pp. 142, 332.

80. Ibid., pp. 298, 308, 354, and *Political Killings*, p. 213.

81. Michael T. Klare and Cynthia Arnson, *Supplying Repression: U.S. Support for Authoritarian Regimes Abroad*, rev. ed. (Washington, D.C.: Institute for Policy Studies, 1981), p. 85.

82. U.S. Congress, *Human Rights and U.S. Foreign Policy*, pp. 80–81, 89–90.

83. Ibid., p. 81.

84. Ibid., p. 35.

85. Ibid., p. 37.

86. U.S. Congress, *Human Rights in Asia: Communist Countries*, p. 1.

87. *Political Killings*, p. 212; *Power and Principle*, p. 126; U.S. Congress, *Human Rights in Asia: Non-Communist Countries*, p. 249.

88. Cohen, "Conditioning U.S. Security Assistance," p. 256, and U.S. Congress, *Human Rights and U.S. Foreign Policy*, p. 157.

89. Brzezinski, *Power and Principle*, p. 127; U.S. Congress, *Human Rights and U.S. Foreign Policy*, p. 298; Atwood, *Plain Talk on Human Rights*, p. 3.

90. The Shultz comments were made in a Peoria, Illinois, address February 22, 1984; for those by Abrams, see U.S. Congress, *Review of U.S. Human Rights Policy*, pp. 3, 5.

91. U.S. Congress, *Review of U.S. Human Rights Policy*, pp. 15–18; Brown, *With Friends Like These*, p. 87; "House Urges Reagan to Drop Liberian Aid," *The New York Times*, February 19, 1986; and *Washington in Focus*, Bulletin on Congressional and Executive Activities Relating to Latin America, Washington Office on Latin America, vol. 3, no. 7 (October 17, 1985), p. 6.

92. Brown, *With Friends Like These*, p. 5; and conversations at the Department of State, September 1985.

4

Actions Taken on Behalf of Human Rights

The third general area where the human rights policies of the Carter and Reagan administrations may be compared is the kinds of efforts they made to give effect to these policies. Policy implementation for both administrations involved the employment of two major types of tactics: (1) diplomatic representations, both private (quiet diplomacy) and public (open diplomacy), and (2) applying pressures and awarding benefits. Both administrations also used two other tactics, which operated more indirectly on national human rights situations: issuing annual country reports on human rights practices and the promotion of democratic institutions and procedures in other countries. The use of these techniques by the two administrations is the focus of this chapter.

QUIET AND OPEN DIPLOMACY

The Carter Administration

Diplomatic procedures constituted one of a number of tactics used by the Carter administration to give effect to its human rights policy. As described by Carter's Human Rights Bureau head, Patricia Derian, such techniques included:

1. We talk: informally, as we have always done, and formally and officially with other governments. When there are abuses, we express our concern. Where there is progress, we support it.
2. We act symbolically. When officials of the U.S. Government travel, we meet with dissidents and with the exiled victims of human rights abuses.
3. We work to strengthen international institutions for the protection of human rights.
4. We give a central place to human rights in our programs of economic aid, [applying] the rule that no aid should be approved for a repressive government unless it directly benefits the poor in such critical areas as food, housing, and medical care.

5. We generally refuse to permit exports of police weapons and equipment to repressive governments.

6. We subject programs of military aid and arms sales to careful, systematic human rights review.[1]

As described by Deputy Secretary of State Warren Christopher, the Carter administration's approach to implementation tactics was that "the most effective strategy for obtaining human rights improvements is one that combines the full range of diplomatic approaches with a willingness to adjust our foreign assistance programs as required. No element in the overall strategy can be as effective alone as in combination with others."[2]

The Carter administration not only included diplomacy in its repertoire of implementation tactics, but also realized the value of both quiet and open, or public diplomacy, and used both techniques. There is ample reason to question the validity of the charge against the Carter administration by one of the Reagan administration's most prominent spokespersons, Jeane Kirkpatrick, who said:

One reason for the failure of the Carter policy was the belief that you can influence governments and people more effectively by hitting them over the head with a two by four, excoriating and humiliating them publicly and treating them as moral pariahs than by using quiet persuasion and diplomacy.[3]

This allegation expressed what a spokesperson for the Lawyers Committee for International Human Rights viewed as

a serious misconception that the Reagan Administration promoted: that the Carter Administration was a loud, raucous group who didn't rely on quiet diplomacy. The opposite was true. We in Nongovernmental Organizations were often critical of the Carter Administration for not being more public more often.[4]

The statement by Kirkpatrick and others in the Reagan administration led Patricia Derian to observe, "I keep hearing the Reagan Administration people say, 'We're going to practice quiet diplomacy,' as though they were inventing the electric light for the first time." Quiet diplomacy, according to a February 1981 comment by Derian,

is actually something that was used in the last four years. What we did in the quiet diplomacy area was put human rights on the official agenda so that we sat across the table and discussed these matters in the same way other bilateral problems are discussed between countries. And we did do that.[5]

In thus denying that there was anything new in the Reagan administration's use of quiet diplomacy, Derian was expressing an opinion that was shared by a State Department official whose career spanned both administrations:

"There was no significant change, from Carter to Reagan, concerning the place of quiet or open diplomacy; both used both tactics."[6] Not only was quiet diplomacy included in the Carter administration's array of implementation tactics, but it held a high place in this list. In the words of one official who served in Carter's Human Rights Bureau,

Carter's preference was to go into a country in discussions by a U.S. ambassador or a special mission and say, "There is a concern about human rights. We are extremely concerned that, given the importance the United States puts on human rights, and the obligations assumed under the UN Charter, if these violations go on, they will affect our relations in a negative way."[7]

The tactical procedure was to start with quiet diplomacy and if this approach was not successful, move on to other techniques. The high status that the Carter administration accorded to quiet diplomacy was sufficiently marked as to merit its inclusion in a list of principles that were seen to constitute a consensus concerning the conduct of its human rights policy. In this list, the sixth item stated, "Though public pressure and direct leverage can be effective instruments of human rights policy, quiet diplomatic efforts and hints of linkage between human rights and U.S. support are often likely to be more effective."[8]

Patricia Derian exemplified the strong reliance on quiet diplomacy by the Carter administration. Of her it was said that "for every case where she was vocal there were ten of quiet diplomacy."[9] She took this approach in such instances as her visits to the Ivory Coast, where she tried to encourage a movement toward democracy; to the Philippines, where President Marcos was warned about the negative place to which history would probably consign him; and to Argentina, where she made strong representations to the president concerning human rights.[10]

Other Carter administration personnel were similarly involved in the use of quiet diplomacy for the promotion of human rights. Secretary of State Cyrus Vance gave expression to his preference for this technique in such experiences as his visit to the shah of Iran, and Vice-President Walter Mondale met in Geneva with South Africa's Prime Minister Vorster to discuss the racial problem in South Africa. "Vigorous and consistent" representations on behalf of the U.S. human rights policy were made to the Marcos government by the American embassy in Manila; the U.S. ambassador took to the successor of the shah of Iran his government's protests concerning the summary executions and widespread human rights violations under the new Iranian regime; and Patricia Derian, replying to questions concerning the U.S. response to the human rights situation in Indonesia, stated that "even when we get descriptions of conditions we aren't certain about, if they raise serious problems, we begin to speak to the government about it."

A final indication of the central place of quiet diplomacy in the Carter administration is the use of this tactic by Carter himself: in a 1979 visit to Seoul, where he expressed his human rights concern to South Korea's President Park; in a 1978 meeting with Andrei Gromyko and other Soviet leaders where he raised the human rights issue as he had in a previous letter to the Soviet leader Leonid Brezhnev; and in his conversations with China's Deng Xiaoping with whom Carter voiced his concern for human rights during a 1979 visit to Washington; Carter requested the Chinese leader to be more flexible in the matter of emigration from China.[11]

While the Carter administration strongly relied on quiet diplomacy for the implementation of its human rights policy, it was also quite willing to go public with its human rights concerns. Secretary Vance expressed the administration's thinking on this point in his statement that "we will speak frankly about injustice both at home and abroad . . . [but] we don't intend to be strident. . . . We will comment when we see a threat to human rights when it is constructive to do so."[12] Deputy Secretary of State Warren Christopher agreed: "In some circumstances a public statement of concern or praise may be appropriate. We generally do not prefer to use public criticism, but we will not shrink from it where it can be effective." Christopher added:

The reason I say we prefer not to use public criticism is that where we have other avenues, we think they are more effective. . . . It is in those situations where we lack a close relationship or an important dialogue that public statements become necessary and the only effective tool.

Cambodia is a good example of a country with which we don't have diplomatic relations but where we are nevertheless terribly concerned about the trend of human rights developments. Under such circumstances, we feel we have to speak out in the hope that other countries, which do have diplomatic relations or which may have some leverage, will make known their views.

At other times public statements are made simply in the hope that the international community will abhor the situation as we do and that there will be a growing feeling that something must be done.[13]

Carter's readiness to resort to open diplomacy when the occasion seemed to call for it was exemplified in his 1979 visit to South Korea, when he publicly expressed his concern for human rights in statements to the press, in a joint commuiniqué, and in his toast at a state dinner, broadcast throughout South Korea;[14] in his outspoken defense of the rights of Soviet dissidents; in the sympathetic letter he wrote to Andrey Sakharov; and in his meeting, at the White House, with another Russian dissident, Vladimir Bukovsky.[15] The human rights abuses in the Soviet Union and Eastern European countries were frequently handled through other forms of public diplomacy, such as the sessions related to the Conference on Security and Cooperation in Europe, where the United States kept pressure on the Soviet Union and its allies in an effort to induce them to comply with the human rights provisions of the Helsinki Accord.

Carter administration people also used open diplomacy in their visits to various countries. While in Argentina, Patricia Derian issued a list of a thousand "disappeareds" and at a press conference demanded an answer from the Argentinian government concerning the fate of these individuals. Andrew Young attended an anti-apartheid conference in Nigeria as a personal representative of President Carter, thereby giving a clear signal of the administration's attitude toward racial segregation in South Africa.[16]

The Carter administration's open diplomacy also involved the use of multilateral channels, principally the United Nations, the Organization of American States, and the Conference on Security and Cooperation in Europe. The procedures of these institutions provided an opportunity for the administration to make its human rights concerns a matter of public record, and the publicity attending their sessions served to amplify the administration's voice as it spoke to human rights situations in various countries.

Testifying to the usefulness of multilateral channels for the implementation of his administration's human rights policy, Deputy Secretary of State Warren Christopher noted, "U.S. delegates had spoken out forcefully on human rights violations in Argentina, Uruguay, and Paraguay during public discussion at the UN and the Organization of American States." Christopher also called attention to the "active participation" of the United States in the sessions held to examine the record of compliance with the human rights provisions of the Helsinki Act, a product of the thirty-five-nation Conference on Security and Cooperation in Europe. In these meetings, said Christopher, the U.S. "has not hesitated" to make public its belief that the Soviet Union and its Eastern European allies were not being faithful to the commitments made under the Helsinki agreement.[17]

In another instance the administration gave "strong support" to a 1980 resolution in the UN's Commission on Human Rights that dealt with human rights violations in Kampuchea (Cambodia). It gave similar backing to another commission resolution that linked rights abuses in Kampuchea with the vast number of refugees fleeing from that country.

Additional evidence of the value that the Carter administration placed on multilateral institutions as channels for open human rights diplomacy is the efforts it made to improve these institutions. As Professor Tom J. Farer observed during a congressional hearing, the administration considered building up such institutions as the Inter-American Commission on Human Rights to be one of its most notable achievements. Among the institutions that the Carter administration sought to strengthen were those that were part of the UN's human rights machinery. Looking toward their improvement, Carter urged more frequent meetings of the Commission on Human Rights and the speeding up of its process for handling complaints of violations; the strengthening of the Human Rights Division's liaison office in New York; the appointment of a high commissioner for human rights; a regular system of consultation among the secretariats of UN agencies whose programs dealt in some way with human rights; improved coordination between the UN and regional human rights organizations; and changes in the UN's calendar that would make the Human Rights Commission's work more effective.

The Reagan Administration

The Reagan administration's approach to the question of tactics to be used to implement its human rights policy was summarized in the introduction to the *Country Reports on Human Rights Practices for 1983*, which noted a "broad range of instruments and techniques."

In dealing with friendly governments, we have engaged in the kind of frank diplomatic exchanges often referred to as "quiet diplomacy." Where diplomatic approaches have not prevailed, or where our influence with a foreign government is minimal, we have dissociated ourselves from odious human rights practices by denying economic and military assistance, voting against multilateral loans, and denying diplomatic support. Where appropriate we have distanced ourselves from human rights violators by public pressures and statements denouncing their actions. In most cases, we have employed a mixture of traditional diplomacy and public affirmation of American interest in the issue.[18]

Diplomatic procedures clearly occupied a prominent place in the catalog of implementation tools, including both quiet and open diplomacy. In contrast to the Carter administration, which was accused of excessive reliance on open diplomacy, Reagan's was criticized for its alleged overdependence on and improper use of quiet diplomacy. The first charge against the Reagan administration was that it practiced quiet diplomacy selectively, failing to employ it in dealing with Soviet Bloc states, Nicaragua, and Cuba. A second criticism was that its most frequent use, in dealings with friendly, authoritarian regimes, failed to produce results. In an appearance before a congressional subcommittee, Elliott Abrams had stated that there had been a considerable improvement in the South African human rights situation as a consequence of U.S. policy, and that South Africa was one of the administration's success stories in its pursuit of quiet diplomacy. This statement was challenged by Millard W. Arnold, who used the same congressional hearing to assert that "the record does not support the claim of Secretary Abrams. . . . There has been a dramatic surge in deaths in detention . . . and torture is on the upswing.[19]

The effectiveness of the Reagan administration's quiet diplomacy approach to human rights situations was seen as being lessened by an absence of a political will to act when its representations were rejected. Consequently, the allegation ran, authoritarian regimes had no reason to fear that their relations with the United States would suffer if they did not respond positively; they would continue to receive arms, advisors, and other forms of U.S. aid. Moreover, according to those critics, these regimes knew that the administration was unwilling to express its concerns openly, and therefore could ignore its private initiatives without fear of being publicly embarrassed. According to this view, the effectiveness of quiet diplomacy depends on a willingness to go public when the private approach fails, and the Reagan administration was not willing to do so.[20]

A third charge against the Reagan administration's quiet diplomacy was that its potential for success was negated by administration actions that conveyed a different, and opposite, message to governments. To support this accusation, critics note that administration representatives met with leaders of a repressive Chilean regime but not with members of the Chilean Human Rights Commission, had dinner with Argentine leaders on the eve of that country's invasion of the Falkland Islands, and met with South African generals.[21] They also note that the administration expressed its intention to deal with the Philippines' human rights problem through quiet diplomacy but then reduced the possibility for success in this approach by such actions as the 1981 visit to Manila by Vice-President Bush, when he publicly praised Filipino President Marcos's "adherence to democratic principles and to the democratic process."[22] Actions such as these could understandably be viewed as public signals of U.S. support for repressive regimes, creating doubts as to how seriously governments should take private representations. Finally, some critics charge that the Reagan administration's quiet diplomacy was actually "silent diplomacy: the muted diplomacy is seen as mute diplomacy . . . [and] our diplomacy is so quiet in this area that most of our ambassadors do not know much about it."[23]

It is safe to assume that the extent and intensity of this criticism of the Reagan administration's quiet diplomacy were prompted by the impression, justified or not, that the administration's human rights diplomacy was confined to this approach. The very strength of the administration's public commitment to quiet diplomacy, in other words, clearly invited a particularly keen scrutiny of this tactic and how it was working in practice.

Equally clear was the administration's belief in the superiority and efficacy of quiet diplomacy as a human rights policy tool. Administration personnel, moreover, took advantage of opportunities as they arose to explain and defend this tactic. Thus, the introduction to the *Country Reports on Human Rights Practices for 1983* contains this statement:

Perhaps the phrase "quiet diplomacy" does not fully convey either the intensity of American efforts, or the depth of our concern, on behalf of human rights victims, yet in many cases, this kind of intercession has proven an effective response to human rights violations. Let us be clear that "quiet" diplomacy refers only to confidentiality of the diplomatic channels we use, not to the intensity of our representations.[24]

Elliott Abrams also expressed the administration's concern to put quiet diplomacy in the most favorable light possible.

Among the advantages of this route are the careful control over it we can exercise; the fact that issues of American arrogance or neocolonialism, or a foreign government's sensitivity to public pressure and to its own sovereignty, are minimized; and the fact that we avoid adding inadvertently to any campaign aimed at delegitimizing or destabilizing the government in question.[25]

The Reagan administration made frequent use of quiet diplomacy, directing it toward a variety of national situations. Elliott Abrams used it, for example, in discussions with officials in Western democracies concerning the persecution, on religious grounds, of the Baha'is in Iran; in contacts with the Soviets on behalf of human rights activists and those who would like to emigrate from the Soviet Union; in discussions with the El Salvadorian government concerning death squads; in Paraguay in talks between the U.S. ambassador and the head of this country's repressive regime; and in South Korea on behalf of imprisoned opposition leader Kim Dac Jung.[26] While quiet diplomacy held a prominent place in the tactics that the Reagan administration used for the implementation of its human rights policy, it also frequently used open diplomacy. There is something both paradoxical and intriguing in this administration's readiness to go public with its human rights concerns, since spokespersons for the administration loudly criticized the Carter administration for its alleged inclination to rely too heavily on open diplomacy and had asserted that the Reagan administration would pursue a different tactical course, suggesting that open diplomacy would have little or no place in the Reagan human rights policy. Moreover, critics of the Reagan administration accused it of an unwillingness to go public concerning human rights violations in other countries, particularly those that were friendly to the United States.

The official version of the Reagan administration's attitude toward open diplomacy was given in this administration's first edition of the *Country Reports on Human Rights Practices* in February 1982. Here the identification of the means to be used in the pursuit of its human rights policy included the statement that "in addition, the human rights policy employs a varied mix of diplomatic tools . . . where private diplomacy is unavailing or unavailable, public statements of concern."[27]

This intention to include open diplomacy for policy implementation was reasserted several years later by the administration's head of the Human Rights Bureau, Elliott Abrams. In the course of a congressional hearing, Abrams was asked to respond to a congressman's statement, "I would hope that your comments [on quiet diplomacy] are not intended to imply that there isn't also a case for public diplomacy." In reply Abrams commented, "I agree completely. Quiet diplomacy cannot be the only arrow in one's quiver; it is one of them. But it's just a tool, not a principle. And . . . there is nothing in what you said . . . that disagrees in any way with our beliefs about this."[28] The Reagan administration thus accepted this instrument as a useful tactic, to be employed when quiet diplomacy could not be, for various reasons, or when governments had proved to be unresponsive to private representations. To this general rule of procedure Abrams added the qualification that the use of this tactic by the executive should be limited.[29]

In view of the Reagan administration's foreign policy focus on the perceived threat of communism in general and the Soviet Union in particular, it is not surprising that much of the administration's public censure of human rights violations was directed toward countries under Communist regimes. It used the forum of the United Nations to denounce the use of torture and politically motivated arrests and detention without trial in Afghanistan; issued a public statement of concern over the prospective trial of a Hungarian dissident publisher, Gabor Demszky; made frequent and strong statements and regularly issued press releases concerning treatment of dissidents and other human rights violations in the Soviet Union; allowed the publication of the warning delivered to Romanian President Nicolae Ceausescu by Secretary of State George P. Shultz that Romania could lose its special trading status with the United States if it did not improve its human rights record; and publicly criticized the human rights records of Nicaragua and Cuba.[30]

Political friends were also subjected to open criticism by the Reagan administration for their human rights failures. Beginning in 1983, for example, the administration steadily intensified its public denunciations of apartheid in South Africa, through such means as the State Department's "detailed and forthright" report on this situation in its annual survey of human rights practices; Under Secretary of State Lawrence Eagleburger's statement that apartheid is "morally wrong" and that "we must reject the legal and political premises and consequences of apartheid"; and the State Department's endorsement of a South African court decision vindicating certain residential rights of blacks in that country.

The Philippine regime of Ferdinand Marcos was another political ally that became an increasingly frequent target of open pressure from the Reagan administration. This change began in 1984, when the administration clearly indicated the importance it attached to the necessity for an impartial and thorough investigation of the assassination of opposition leader Benigno S. Aquino, Jr. The administration was equally clear in its expression of concern that the 1984 election for the Filipino national legislature be "free and fair." Public pressure on the Marcos regime continued to be applied with increasing strength up to the time of Marcos's fall from power, a development to which the Reagan administration made a substantial contribution. In regard to Turkey, another U.S. ally, the Reagan administration resorted to open diplomacy through such actions as U.S. Ambassador Robert Strausz-Hupe's public criticism of the banning of political parties and U.S. Consul General Daniel Newberry's attendance at the trial of publisher Nadir Nadi.

Open diplomacy was practiced to a considerable extent in the case of Iran's treatment of the Baha'i religious community. Specific steps included support of resolutions in the UN's Commission on Human Rights; a State Department press release denouncing the arrest and execution of members of the Baha'i National Spiritual Assembly and the general pattern of suppression of which these acts were a part; a press conference comment by Elliott Abrams calling the correspondents' attention to the "increasingly desperate" situation of the Baha'is in Iran; and a statement by President Reagan asking world leaders to join him in condemning Iran for its persecution of the Baha'is.

A final example is Uganda, which Elliott Abrams publicly denounced during a 1984 congressional hearing. In his testimony Abrams called the Ugandan human rights situation "among the most grave in the world" and blamed the situation to a significant extent on that country's "demoralized, underpaid, and underfed" army.[31]

As these cases indicate, various members of the Reagan administration practiced open diplomacy. The President's December 11, 1985, International Human Rights Day speech is another example. He gave particular emphasis to human rights violations in Communist countries, condemning Vietnam's "vicious attacks" on Cambodian refugees; Ethiopia's "use of famine to punish large segments of its own population"; Poland's continued ban on independent trade unions; Romania's religious persecution; Bulgaria's "repression of the Turkish minority and the Islamic faith"; Cuba, as "the Western Hemisphere's worst example of the country where institutionalized totalitarianism has consistently violated the rights of its citizens"; and Nicaragua, whose Sandinista regime "seems determined to embark on the same course."

While Communist regimes bore the brunt of Reagan's public strictures, some of his critical remarks did deal with several of the many friendly authoritarian systems that were generally conceded to be serious violators of human rights. "In Chile and the Philippines, too," he said, "we have shown our strong concern with our friends who deviate from a strongly established democratic tradition," and he denounced South Africa's "inhuman policy of apartheid," the granting of "essentially unlimited powers" to the police and the arrest of thousands of South Africans who were "denied even elementary judicial protection," and expressed impatience with that country's government, saying that "apartheid is abhorrent" and that "it was time that the Government of South Africa took steps to end it."

The Reagan speech also included a reference to what he termed "Iran's rampant religious persecution" of the Baha'i community, citing statistics concerning members of this faith who had been executed, imprisoned, made homeless, or forced to flee to other countries.[32]

An example of the practice of open diplomacy by a U.S. ambassador representing the Reagan administration is the conduct of Arthur Davis in Paraguay, who made his embassy's concern for rights abuses a matter of public knowledge through such actions as attendance by embassy personnel at a barbecue for the staff of a newspaper that had been forced to cease publication and at a court trial dealing with a significant human rights case.[33] Thomas Pickering was another U.S. ambassador who demonstrated a willingness to go public with a human rights concern. Speaking as his country's representative in El Salvador, Ambassador Pickering delivered a speech in San Salvador in which he decried the lack of governmental activity "against those who murder and kidnap university professors, doctors, labor leaders, *campesinos* and government workers. We know by their selection of victims . . . [that they] are not guerrilla organizations." He was thus holding the El Salvador government responsible for the activities of death squads.[34]

Two other administration leaders resorting to open diplomacy were Vice-President Bush and Secretary of State Shultz, who, while visiting El Salvador, publicly denounced the use of death squads by that country's government.[35]

Like its predecessor, the Reagan administration found occasion to pursue its open diplomacy through multilateral channels. "Multilateral organizations," said Secretary of State Shultz, "are another instrument of our human rights policy." In elaborating on this point, the secretary cited U.S. participation in the work of the UN Commission on Human Rights, the Helsinki (Conference on Security and Cooperation in Europe) process, and the Inter-American Commission on Human Rights.[36]

As an example of the administration's use of UN proceedings to give public expression to its human rights concerns, U.S. spokespersons made representations in 1983 concerning psychiatric abuse of political prisoners, religious intolerance, and the need for multilateral cooperation in the fight against disappearances, political killings, and unlawful forms of detention. These actions in the Commission on Human Rights and the General Assembly's Third Committee were followed by a similar performance, the following year, by UN Deputy Representative Richard Schifter and his associates, whose speeches were directed against religious intolerance, unlawful forms of detention, harsh treatment of political prisoners, and restraints on freedom of expression. In 1985 U.S. Ambassador Vernon A. Walters and other members of the American delegation continued to express concern for these issues.

In addition to vocally expressing U.S. concern for certain human rights issues, Reagan administration personnel took other steps to make its position on certain human rights questions a matter of public record. Thus in 1983 it gave support to the creation of a special fund to aid the victims of torture and their families. In 1984 the U.S. delegation actively promoted the draft Convention Against Torture and Other Cruel, Inhuman or Degrading Treatment or Punishment, and in 1985 the United States gave further backing to both these projects. Illustrative of other forms of open human rights diplomacy through the UN were actions in reference to Iran's persecution of the

Baha'i religious community: cooperation with efforts to involve the UN's Secretary General in endeavors to end this practice and support of resolutions dealing with the Iranian situation.[37]

In keeping with its controlling foreign policy focus, the Reagan administration's open diplomacy at the UN tended to convey criticism of the Soviet Union and other Communist systems and support for governments friendly to the United States. Thus one report on the administration's performance at the UN in 1983 stated:

Ambassador Jeane Kirkpatrick and her aides continued to use the United Nations as a platform for singling out human rights violations in the Soviet Union and Cuba and defending the record of the allies of the United States, including a number of governments that flagrantly abuse their own citizens.

Furthermore, according to this report, in the same UN session the United States "continued to take a strong position in support of UN action on Afghanistan, Poland, Iran, and Kampuchea [while opposing] any actions on Guatemala, El Salvador, and Chile."[38] A similar study two years later concluded:

Despite a lesser degree of U.S. opposition to resolutions on El Salvador and Guatemala, the performance of the Reagan Administration in the UN with respect to these countries did not reflect a substantial change in 1985. . . . As in previous years, the U.S. delegation voted against resolutions on the human rights situation in Chile.[39]

PRESSURES AND INDUCEMENTS

In addition to resorting to quiet and/or open diplomacy for the implementation of its human rights policy, an administration may take another form of direct action in an effort to influence a human rights situation in another country: a combination of rewards and punishments. More popularly known as the "carrot-and-stick" approach, this technique involves the promise of benefits to a government that improves its human rights performance and/or the threat of sanctions if it does not.

In practical terms, this policy approach focuses on U.S. military and economic aid, arms and military equipment sales, and such other tangible concerns as the opportunity for and terms of trade, and seeks to make these transactions contingent on a particular country's human rights record. In applying this technique, an administration may proceed on a bilateral basis, dealing directly with another government in dispensing favors or applying sanctions, or indirectly, through such multilateral channels as international financial institutions (IFIs).

Particular significance attaches to the IFIs as pressure/inducement channels, since most countries attach more importance to them as sources of capital than to U.S. bilateral aid. Moreover, the presence of IFIs somewhat diminishes the effectiveness of U.S. bilateral aid as a pressure/inducement device, since countries threatened by this tactic can turn to the IFIs for the assistance they need.

For these and other reasons, IFIs have themselves become attractive arenas in and through which the U.S. could employ its pressure/inducement tactic in regard to human rights situations in certain countries. Implicit in this procedure is the belief that the outcome of IFIs' decisions on pending loans can have an effect on the human rights behavior of the recipients of such aid, and, more important from a U.S. standpoint, that the United States is capable of influencing the nature of these decisions. The validity of the key part of this thesis has been challenged by those who point to "the absolute failure of U.S. opposition votes on human rights grounds to stop a single loan from being granted by the multilateral development banks (MDBs)." The use of IFIs to achieve American human rights objectives has also been criticized as a politicizing of the procedures of institutions whose charters require them to make decisions on economic grounds only.

On the positive side of the question of using IFIs as channels for U.S. human rights pressure tactics, it has been argued that the effectiveness of this technique does not depend on the ability to determine the outcome of votes on proposed loans. Thus, according to Ralph Dungan, U.S. executive director of the Inter-American Development Bank,

Even when a vote passes, there is a price to pay for one or more negative votes or even an abstention. The country pays a price in terms of its public relations, and indeed sometimes its financial situation. . . . If there is some indication that . . . it has difficulties sufficient to cause a member of one of these banks to either abstain or vote "no," that becomes a serious problem for the banking authorities of that country.[40]

As to the second objection that using IFIs as channels for human rights pressure tactics would politicize them, one answer has been the belief that this danger can be avoided, or at least minimized, by using economic, rather than human rights arguments to support U.S. objections to certain loans. This can be easily done "with enough time and effort, an arguable technical position can be developed in either direction on virtually any proposal in the IFIs." While such subterfuges can be easily contrived, however, they can just as easily be seen for what they are: not too subtle substitutes for the real reasons underlying a policy position.[41]

Regardless of the pros and cons of bringing IFIs into the picture of human rights pressure/inducement tactics, this was done, and the performance of the Carter and Reagan administrations in regard to this and other carrot/stick devices will be discussed in this part of the chapter.

The Carter Administration

Some doubt apparently existed in the minds of Carter administration personnel and of some of the State Department people with whom the administration had to work concerning the usefulness of sanctions as a device to effect changes in the human rights behavior of another government. Patricia Derian's testimony before a congressional committee on the subject of the situation in the Philippines, for example, included her opinion that a threat to withhold security assistance from this country would not produce a change in that situation. In a more general statement of her attitude toward this tactic, Derian stated:

I don't favor the carrot and stick approach to human rights. I think it doesn't work. I don't think you can buy people out of jail without insuring and guaranteeing that the next time whatever it is you bought them with is wanted. And 5,000 innocent people wind up sitting in the cooler until you deliver the next installment. I don't think that works.[42]

Two officials serving in the State Department during the Carter administration expressed similar skepticism. One, Michael Armacost, said:

If you begin to make that kind of direct linkage [between military assistance and human rights conditions] and say we will cut military assistance unless Country X does these . . . things, I have serious doubts as to whether that kind of explicit linkage is effective.[43]

Relating the question of sanctions to the specific issue of linking the sale of "dual-use" technology to the human rights situation in China, another member of the State Department, Charles W. Freeman, stated that he did not believe that the withholding of this equipment would have "any significant effect whatsoever on the human rights process in China."[44]

Despite these negative opinions concerning the usefulness of the pressure/inducement approach to human rights policy implementation, Deputy Secretary of State Warren Christopher, speaking for the Carter administration, could say, "We are prepared to support our words with actions . . . to take tangible steps to recognize good human rights performance or to manifest our concern over human rights violations." The "tangible steps" to which he referred had to do with this country's foreign assistance programs, which were to be made subject to human rights considerations.[45]

The Carter administration evidently took this commitment to take "tangible steps" in support of its human rights policy and to apply sanctions if and when necessary seriously. Patricia Derian testified to a congressional subcommittee hearing that foreign military sales programs had been reduced in 1980 for South Korea, Indonesia, and Zaire, all with poor human rights records. In the preceding year, as deputy secretary of state Warren Christopher noted, a concern for human rights conditions had led to the postponement or elimination of aid programs for Nicaragua, Afghanistan, and Ethiopia; the reduction of assistance levels for El Salvador, the Central African Empire, the Philippines, Paraguay, Uruguay, Guinea, and Chile; and the cessation of military sales to Argentina. On the "carrot" side of the reward/punishment strategy, assistance levels had been raised for seven countries with improved human rights records: India, Sri Lanka, Botswana, the Gambia, Costa Rica, the Dominican Republic, and Peru. The application of sanctions against Argentina was accompanied by a program of graduated rewards that could follow improvements in the area of human rights.[46] Cases such as these led one observer to conclude that "to the extent that the Carter administration was successful in defending human rights it was because Carter was willing, although on a very limited basis, to employ financial and economic sanctions as a last resort."[47]

While the Carter administration was willing to use the pressure/inducement tactic, its employment of this technique met some negative evaluation. One such criticism concerned the administration's alleged refusal to use import and export trade restrictions as an instrument to defend human rights. Stephen B. Cohen found the administration to have exhibited "a remarkable degree of tentativeness and caution" in its application of Section 502B of the amended Foreign Assistance Act of 1961, which forbade assistance to any government that displayed a consistent pattern of gross violations of internationally recognized human rights. According to Cohen, "relatively few governments" were found guilty of such abusive performance, and "security assistance was actually cut off to even fewer."[48]

Any review of the Carter administration's use of the pressure/inducement tactic must take into consideration the fact that this, like all aspects of the administration's human rights policy, felt the impact of the bureaucratic conflict that the Carter commitment to human rights precipitated. One result of this struggle was the exclusion of important segments of the total U.S. foreign assistance program from review by the Interagency Group on Human Rights and Foreign Assistance (the "Christopher Group"). This exclusion, in turn, limited the administration's ability to employ the carrot/stick approach in the implementation of its human rights policy, since so much of it involves aid programs. The exemption of a number of these programs from Christopher Group review thus deprived the administration of some of the policy instruments through which pressure could be brought to bear on governments on behalf of human rights.

Of the aid programs withdrawn from Christopher Group review because of pressures from within the bureaucracy, the two "largest and diplomatically most potent" were military assistance and the Security Supporting Assistance, or, as it was known after 1979, the Economic Support Fund. These two were dropped from the Christopher Group's agenda at the insistence of

Undersecretary for Security Assistance Lucy Benson, who, determined to resist any move that would lessen her authority, threatened to resign if the two programs in question were not exempt from group review. Benson's successful defense of her bureaucratic turf made it more difficult for the administration to use certain aid programs for human rights purposes. This did not, however, altogether close the door on this tactic, since the Human Rights Bureau was a member of Benson's Security Assistance Program Review Working Group and its institutional parent, the Arms Export Control Board. The bureau, moreover, was given the right to appeal Benson's decisions on military and security aid, in these two agencies, to Deputy Secretary of State Christopher.

Another participant in the bureaucratic conflict that succeeded in winning exemption of its programs from Christopher Group review was the Department of Agriculture. This department's victory affected the three principal food aid programs: concessionary sales to governments under the Food for Peace program; donations to relief organizations and governments for relief and food-for-work under the same program; and export credits through the Commodity Credit Corporation. Here, again, while the administration's ability to use aid programs as a pressure/inducement tool was considerably weakened, it was not completely lost, thanks to a Christopher-formulated compromise. Under this compromise, the Agriculture Department was required to demonstrate that the proceeds from concessionary sales to any country having human rights problems would be used for the benefit of its needy people. As Caleb Rossiter has pointed out, this meant that a "clear message would be delivered to a government, that the United States felt it had 'problems.'

Two other components in the total U.S. aid program were also involved in the process of diluting the Christopher Group's review power: development assistance, administered by the Agency for International Development, and the commercial programs carried on through the Export-Import Bank and the Overseas Private Investment Corporation. In these program areas, as in the two already noted, some human rights impact was preserved through compromise formulas. The net effect of the outcome of the bureaucratic struggle involving development assistance and commercial programs, however, was to add two more names to the list of foreign policy tools that could be used to only a limited extent for pressure/inducement purposes.[49] Caleb Rossiter described these developments in regard to the place of human rights in U.S. aid programs as a "fateful transition of the Christopher Group from a forum reviewing all aid decisions to one primarily reviewing U.S. positions on multilateral bank (MDB) proposals." This outcome of the bureaucratic conflict within the Carter administration, according to Rossiter, traced to the fact that:

the MDBs were the channel of U.S. assistance least protected by a sponsor in the executive branch, and were unable to gain the exemption from the Christopher Group achieved by the bilateral programs and the International Monetary Fund. By default they were to be the focus of the Christopher Group and, because of the time and bureaucratic symbolism invested in that body, of human rights policy as well.[50]

There were paradoxical elements in this emergence of international financial institutions (IFIs) as a pressure/inducement tool for the implementation of the Carter human rights policy. First, IFIs are far less amenable to control by an administration, and hence less attractive as policy-implementation instruments, than are bilateral aid programs. Second, the Carter administration had initially sought to prevent legislation that would have required U.S. representatives to MDBs to oppose loans to countries with poor human rights records. In support of its position, the administration argued that mandating this kind of action by American representatives would politicize the MDBs, whose decisions were to be based on economic considerations only, and would deprive this country's representatives of the flexibility they needed for effective implementation of U.S. policy in the IFIs.

In place of the congressional action it opposed, the Carter administration was party to a substitute provision stipulating that the U.S. government, by its vote and voice in MDB decisions should advance the cause of human rights by seeking to channel assistance away from countries whose governments exhibited a consistent pattern of gross violations of internationally recognized human rights. This language was subsequently embodied in the opening paragraph and following subsection of Section 701 of the International Financial Institutions Act of 1977. The Carter administration's effort to blunt legislation that would have more tightly bound the actions of U.S. representatives to MDBs was also successful, for the 1977 legislation did not directly instruct these representatives to vote "no" on proposed loans to human rights violators: Subsection (f) merely stipulates that they are to "oppose" loans or financial or technical assistance to such countries. This requirement, however, does not apply in the case of assistance "directed specifically to programs which serve the basic human needs" of the citizens of these countries.

Despite its early resistance to congressional efforts to compel the administration's representative to use IFIs for the implementation of this country's human rights policy, the Carter administration did, in fact, use these institutions for this purpose. While it had initially argued against "politicizing" the IFIs, the administration spoke through Treasury Secretary Michael Blumenthal as he told a congressional subcommittee in 1979:

I see absolutely nothing wrong with urging the banks to pay attention to giving more money to those who meet basic human needs than to those that do not, to looking less kindly upon those who have minimum regard for human rights. . . . I think it is entirely appropriate for us to say that we are opposed to providing aid to a country that we feel is so egregious in its violation of how it treats its people that we cannot sit still without losing our influence.[51]

As a further indication of its willingness to employ IFIs as a means by which pressure could be brought to bear upon human rights violators, the Carter administration gave a broad interpretation to the word "oppose" in the legislation governing U.S. representatives to these institutions. According to Secretary Blumenthal, the administration considered "oppose" to mean any action except an affirmative vote. The United States could thus register its opposition to a particular loan simply by abstaining.

Either through abstentions or "no" votes, the Carter administration opposed 117 proposed loans on human rights grounds during its term in office, voting "no" in 41 cases. This kind of pressure on behalf of human rights was brought to bear in four different institutions: the World Bank, including the International Development Association and the International Finance Corporation; the Asian Development Bank; the African Development Bank; and the Inter-American Development Bank. The proposed loans that the United States opposed related to seventeen different countries, nine of which were targets of "no" votes by U.S. representatives: Afghanistan, Argentina, Chile, Equatorial Guinea, Laos, Mozambique, Paraguay, Uruguay, and Vietnam. The other countries to which the United States sought to deny financial assistance were Benin, the Central African Republic, El Salvador, Ethiopia, Guinea, South Korea, the Philippines, and the People's Democratic Republic of Yemen. From this list it is apparent that the Carter administration was proceeding on an evenhanded basis in seeking to use IFI action to induce countries with poor human rights records to improve their performance. This balanced application of pressure through IFIs was emphasized by the administration's 1977 voting record in MDBs. In that year, the United States voted eighteen times against loans to nine governments that the Christopher Group had identified as rights violators; of these, four were leftist regimes (Benin, Central African Republic, Ethiopia, and Guinea) and five were right-wing regimes: Argentina, Chile, South Korea, the Philippines, and Uruguay.

The evenhandedness of the Carter administration's actions in IFIs is further demonstrated in statistics concerning the value of loans to which these actions related. These figures show that the administration opposed loans constituting 34 percent of the total loans under consideration for leftist countries and 31 percent of those involving rightist nations.[52]

Votes on proposed loans were not the only way in which the Carter administration sought to use IFIs as a pressure/inducement instrument. This point was made by Assistant Treasury Secretary G. Fred Bergsten, who, in explaining how the administration's human rights policy was applied through these institutions, stated:

Our overall human rights policy has many aspects, and when we decide to vote against a loan in a development bank, we don't just vote and that is it. The State Department calls in the ambassador of that country . . . and tells him what is coming up and why. Our ambassador in that country tells them what is coming and why.

Our Executive Director [in the involved bank] tells the Executive Director for that country . . . what is coming and why.[53]

Through its votes and other actions in the IFIs, the Carter administration compiled a record of performance in relation to Section 701 of the International Financial Institutions Act that led a spokesperson for the Lawyers Committee for International Human Rights to conclude, "that section and other similar provisions were enforced steadily and faithfully during the Carter years." The positive attitude thus demonstrated by the administration toward this human rights legislation stands in contrast to the original Carter opposition to it, on the grounds that its mandated action in IFIs deprived the administration of the flexibility it needed for the effective conduct of its human rights policy. Bergsten expressed later administration thinking on this subject in his observation:

It has been my feeling . . . that we have been able to succeed in taking the present legislative language and fitting it into our own policy on human rights, without undermining the integrity of the multilateral process.[54]

It may indeed be true that the "integrity of the multilateral process" and the nonpolitical character of IFIs were preserved even while the Carter administration was using them as pressure/inducement instruments. If so, two aspects of U.S. procedure that Rossiter noted may have been responsible. U.S. representatives never stated in meetings of these institutions' governing bodies that they were voting "no" or abstaining for human rights reasons, nor did they put pressure on MDBs or their members to defeat or delay loans that the United States opposed.[55]

This unwillingness to apply pressure in the IFIs was seen as reflecting credit on the Carter administration's performance, though those who would prefer a more aggressive approach to the matter of protecting human rights through these institutions would undoubtedly dispute this conclusion. Negative critics of the Carter administration's handling of human-rights-related issues in the IFIs would also point to its support of loans to Guatemala and Zaire, and to the fact that it never actually designated any country as showing a consistent pattern of gross violations of internationally recognized human rights.

The Reagan Administration

In the opinion of Human Rights Bureau head Elliott Abrams and presumably that of the Reagan administration, "proper human rights policy" consists of terminating economic assistance to countries where there are continuing problems and of withholding from them such benefits as diplomatic support, votes for multilateral loans, crime control equipment, and military assistance and training. Specific human rights policy instruments like these, according to Abrams, "have an important place in an integrated policy, and the Reagan Administration has used them along with other methods of diplomacy."

Abrams also expressed this attitude toward the use of the pressure/inducement tactic in testimony before a congressional subcommittee, adding that the administration was using the tools at its disposal to deny economic assistance, vote against multilateral loans, and deny export of munitions and crime control and detection equipment. In another statement indicative of the Reagan administration's willingness to see pressures applied in human rights situations, Abrams expressed the administration's support for House and Senate resolutions calling on the U.S. government to cease all commercial relations with Iran, where the Baha'i religious community was being persecuted.[56]

The "carrot" part of the pressure/inducement tactic was also part of the Reagan administration's program for the implementation of its human rights policy. Early in its life Rita Hauser, U.S. representative to the UN's Commission on Human Rights, expressed the expectation that the Reagan administration use this positive approach to human rights situations. Speaking on the specific subject of U.S. policy toward South Africa, Hauser said:

We would sit down with South Africa's leaders and say, "You want to be part of the Western Alliance? You've got to make certain concessions now, major changes in your policy of apartheid, which is unacceptable to the rest of the Western world" and use it as a carrot to bring them in rather than denounce them.[57]

Evidence that Hauser was correct in her assumption that the carrot approach would be part of the Reagan administration's human rights strategy came in the administration's use of the concept of improved human rights records as a justification for U.S. aid to certain governments. The official rationale for this procedure was that American recognition of improvement in a particular government's human rights performance would encourage further progress. This recognition could be extended through such channels as the State Department's annual review of countries' human rights practices and votes in multilateral development banks.

This "carrot" of recognizing improvement was exemplified in President Reagan's efforts in 1985 to induce the rebels fighting the Sandinista government in Nicaragua to put an end to the human rights abuses attributed to them. Since these alleged violations figured prominently in the congressional debate over continued aid to the insurgents, the president was, in effect, telling the rebels that their chances of receiving help from the United States would be stronger if they improved their human rights performance.[58]

One aspect of the Reagan administration's pressure/inducement tactic that aroused particularly strong negative criticism was its performance under the legislation that called for opposition in IFIs to loans to countries showing a consistent pattern of gross violation of internationally recognized human rights. In one such negative evaluation of this administration's performance, Caleb Rossiter observed:

During Carter's term, the multilateral banks were the focus of human rights policy. Since then, however, the Reagan Administration has all but abandoned the use of votes in the MDBs as a primary tool of human rights policy. In the banks, the United States now opposes only left-wing governments on human rights grounds. It no longer opposes loans to right-wing governments allied to U.S. interests no matter what their degree of human rights abuses. With this dichotomy, the United States is perceived as forsaking a balanced pursuit of human rights in favor of strengthening immediate ties with allies and weakening unsympathetic regimes.[59]

Such critical comments were inspired by an attitude on the part of the Reagan administration that had its first expression very early in its term in office. In February 1981 the U.S. representatives to IFIs were directed to discontinue the practice of opposing loans to Argentina, Chile, Uruguay, and Paraguay on human rights grounds. Although these countries were still generally considered to be guilty of offenses against human rights, the administration claimed that the "dramatic improvement" in these countries' human rights performances justified a reversal of the U.S. position on IFI loans to them. The administration also early reversed the previous negative stance in regard to IFI assistance to the Philippines, Guatemala, South Africa, South Korea, El Salvador, and Uruguay.

While the Reagan administration thus moved quickly to end this country's opposition to IFI loans to countries politically allied with the United States, whatever their human rights records, it was equally prompt in demonstrating willingness to use IFIs as a means to bring pressure to bear on left-wing countries that were seen as unfriendly. In so doing, the administration cited human rights violations as the reason for opposing IFI aid to Angola, Syria, Benin, South Yemen, Laos, and Vietnam.

The absence of evenhandedness in the Reagan administration's votes in IFIs on human rights grounds appears again in the administration's overall voting record in IFIs during the first three years of its life. The United States opposed loans that constituted 31 percent of the total value of those considered for leftist countries, while seeking to deny right-wing regimes of only 3 percent of the value of the aid that could accrue to them.

This pattern of selective application of pressure on human rights violators through IFIs continued in the later years of the Reagan administration. In the first nine months of 1985, the United States gave support for loans to at least eight countries guilty of serious rights violations: the Philippines, Turkey, Guatemala, Paraguay, South Korea, Haiti, Pakistan, and El Salvador, all friends of the United States. The only countries to which the administration tried to deny IFI aid were three who were under leftist regimes:

Angola, Syria, and South Yemen. In the period from October 1984 through March 1985, the United States opposed nine loans involving five countries, only one of which (Chile) belonged in the U.S. political camp. Over the same period, administration support was given for thirty-one loans to eight friendly right-wing governments with poor human rights records.

Reagan administration personnel frequently cited improvements in the human rights performance of friendly right-wing regimes as a justification for not using IFI loans as a pressure device against them. This alleged progress meant that these countries were not to be considered as showing a "consistent pattern" of abuses; hence, there was no reason to apply the sanctions that the human rights legislation called for. Thus, in explaining the administration's reversal of U.S. voting patterns in IFIs in regard to Chile, Paraguay, Uruguay, and Argentina, Deputy Assistant Secretary of State Stephen Bosworth commented, "It's our judgment that . . . the trend is one of improvement. . . . So we would not find this a consistent pattern at this time of gross violations."[60] This kind of reasoning did not convince some congressmen; Representative Jim Leach observed:

This thinking is as if one were to argue in the case of Nazi Germany that the closing of Dachau and Auschwitz, while leaving Buchenwald open, would represent a sufficient improvement to warrant a legal determination that a consistent pattern of gross violations no longer existed.[61]

Congressional reaction to this kind of application of the "consistent pattern" criterion in Section 701 of the International Financial Institutions Act of 1977 led to the passage in November 1983 of a supplemental appropriations bill that included the deletion of the word "consistent" from Section 701. Whether because of this congressional action or for other reasons, some changes were noticed in the Reagan administration's pattern of voting in IFIs. Benin, for example, was removed from the list of leftist-ruled countries to whom the United States had consistently sought to deny IFI loans on human rights grounds, and loans to Uganda and Chile were opposed, also on the basis of human rights records. The refusal to support a loan to Chile was the first instance of a Reagan administration application of Section 701 to a right-wing government.

Reagan administration personnel denied that these voting pattern shifts constituted a drastic departure from a previous practice of failure to apply Section 701 and thus use IFIs to implement a human rights policy. Replying to the charge that the administration's votes in IFIs were not responsive to the human rights concerns expressed by Congress and in pertinent legislation, David C. Mulford, assistant secretary of the treasury for international affairs, stated in a congressional hearing:

I would draw your attention to the fact that . . . there have been a number of abstentions in certain of the cases . . . you are referring to. . . . In some cases an abstention can be a reasonably negative expression. So I wouldn't say that there has been an unending and unvariable record of positive votes that are entirely unresponsive.[62]

A defense of the Reagan administration's performance in IFIs could cite one element in its voting record in reply to the charge that it had failed to use these institutions to bring pressure to bear on friendly governments. Thus, through March 1985, the administration had used abstentions, assumed to express opposition, in relation to fifty-one loans involving human rights considerations. These loans related to eleven countries, five of which (Bolivia, Chile, Guatemala, Paraguay, and the Philippines) were generally regarded as friendly to the United States.

In comments that could be construed as an additional defense of the Reagan administration's performance in the IFIs, Elliott Abrams expressed doubts concerning the usefulness of these institutions as channels through which countries could be pressured into better human rights behavior. He voiced this opinion, for example, during a congressional hearing on the particular case of Zaire.

The Carter Administration voted for every single loan to Zaire. That is not because the officials of the Carter Administration, from the President on down, didn't care about the human rights situation in Zaire. That is ridiculous. They did it, presumably, because they determined that it was not an effective way to have influence on human rights in Zaire to vote against the loans, rather there were other ways in which they tried to have influence. We have reached the same conclusion.[63]

OTHER ACTIONS ON BEHALF OF HUMAN RIGHTS

Two other tactics are available to effect changes in the human rights practices of other governments: the annual publication of the *Country Reports on Human Rights Practices* mandated in 1976 by Congress, and taking measures to encourage the development of democratic institutions and practices in other countries.

The Annual Country Reports

The annual State Department reports on the human rights practices of other countries, which now cover all nations, occupy a prominent place in U.S. human rights policy for several reasons, one being that the very requirement that they be prepared and published provides a kind of insurance against the possibility that a particular administration may feel inclined to ignore this element in American foreign policy.

The annual reports are important, furthermore, because of their potential impact on other governments. Foreign government personnel are aware that U.S. embassy people are gathering information for the annual surveys, and their awareness that this process will eventuate in a widely circulated report occasionally leads them to take certain corrective steps, hoping thereby to gain a better press. As several past and present State Department officials have observed, no government likes to be criticized publicly; "many of their leaders are as self-conscious as adolescents, and don't like bad publicity." Consequently, governments are vulnerable to the impact of the country reports because their content becomes public property around the world, read by officials in the governments of other nations.[64]

The annual reports that the Carter administration issued were based on information from a wide variety of sources, the foremost of which was U.S. embassies. Other sources included reports of nongovernmental and intergovernmental human rights organizations, findings of congressional committees, U.S. citizens and visitors from abroad, overseas trips by State Department officials, and the public media. These reports received considerable negative criticism, including allegations that the people who wrote the embassy reports were of low calibre; that there were not enough people available to do the job well; that embassy people involved in the process were not in contact with the society with which they were dealing; and that the debate over material that might lessen the seriousness of certain abuses produced compromises that reflected inter-bureau negotiation rather than consistent policy.

Carter administration personnel acknowledged that there were imperfections in the reports and variations in their quality from country to country and from year to year. Human Rights Bureau head Patricia Derian granted that the reports "were not all perfect"; she also asserted, however, that "they are thorough. They may not have everything in them that other people— or I—would like to see in them, but they are honorable reports, done with integrity and with a care for facts. . . . I have no apologies for these reports . . . [and] I reject out of hand the criticism that we have tried to mislead or be nonobjective."[65] That this claim to objectivity was not simply special pleading is suggested by the conclusion reached on this point by a Congressional Research Service study:

As a result of this process [of debate and negotiation over the content of reports] the data, reports, and allegations on which the country reports are based are exposed to numerous competing views in such a way as to protect against blatant bias or the parochial perspectives of a particular bureau.[66]

The reports produced by the Reagan administration had the same types of information sources as did those under Carter, but they differed in two major ways. They did not include economic/social rights, as such, substituting a section on the "economic, social, and cultural situation" in each country, and the introductory section of the early editions was used to set forth the administration's philosophy concerning human rights.

Like those of the Carter administration, the Reagan country reports encountered negative criticism. Some were said to have been tailored to serve the administration's political purposes, leading to such alleged perversions of the process as the exoneration from blame for abuses those leaders of foreign governments who were friendly to the United States. Some critics also saw political motivation as leading to such distortions as the effort to demonstrate that certain "favored" countries had improved their human rights performance, and to do this by comparing a current situation with long-gone periods when rights abuses were particularly excessive.

In defense of the country reports, Reagan administration personnel asserted that much of the criticism was "misguided" and that those who prepared the reports tried to be unbiased. Supporters of this claim note that in the annual letters sent to ambassadors concerning the preparation of reports, no attempt was made to dictate the content of any report. Instead, the ambassadors were specifically instructed to get all the information asked for and let the reports speak for themselves.[67]

A counterbalance to this negative criticism came from the International Human Rights Law Group in its comments on the 1982 reports:

Although one may find deficiencies in the tone of the country reports and in omissions of particular events and nuances in policies and language that we do not all agree upon, the fact that the Bureau of Human Rights . . . has published a compendious, authoritative, and on the whole conclusive and fair statement of the conduct of foreign governments in their handling of human rights problems is to the complimented.[68]

The Promotion of Democracy

A final kind of action by the two administrations for the implementation of their human rights policies was the promotion of democracy in other countries. This tactic was employed on the assumption that democratic institutions and procedures provide the most certain assurance that people's rights will be respected.

When U.S. administration personnel speak of promoting and protecting human rights by encouraging and assisting the development of democracy, they are talking in terms of their own country's style of democracy, a significant component of which is a concept of representative government that defines representation in terms of legal, formal processes. Narrow and superficial though this version of democracy and political processes may be, it is still the one meant in this discussion of the efforts of the Carter and Reagan administrations to promote human rights by encouraging the development of democracy in other nations. The extent to which such efforts constituted a form of political cultural imperialism and an expression of political ethnocentrism is a question whose answer will obviously vary from individual to individual.

The Carter Administration assumed the link between democracy and human rights. Carter recognized this linkage when he declared in his 1980 State of the Union address, that "we will continue to support the growth of democracy and human rights." This administration apparently operated on the assumption that the promotion of democracy abroad was a desirable and legitimate part of U.S. foreign policy, without emphasizing the fact that its inclusion could be an effective way to advance the cause of human rights.

Carter's concern for the development of democracy abroad found practical expression in steps taken to build democratic institutions in other countries. His commitment to this course of action appeared, for example, in a 1979 speech in which he asserted that "in distributing the scarce resources of our foreign assistance programs, we will demonstrate that our deepest affinities are with nations which commit themselves to a democratic path of development."[69] In carrying out this commitment, the Carter administration used Agency for International Development (AID) resources, with particular attention to African nations. Here institution building involved financial support for such projects as conferences and seminars on justice and its administration and programs like the training of rural magistrates in Zimbabwe and aid to the Botswana court system. Evidencing her own and her administration's interest in institution-building activities of this nature, Patricia Derian visited Africa and encouraged U.S. embassies there to think of ways of using AID funds for this purpose.

The importance that the Carter administration attached to democratic institutions was also expressed in its use of diplomatic channels to apply pressure on certain regimes to move toward democracy. Weekly visits to President Marcos by the U.S. ambassador to the Philippines were the occasion for delivering a continuing message that the return to democratic government in the Philippines was essential for the relief of tensions between the Philippines and the United States and for the stability and welfare of the Philippines.

The Carter administration's interest in helping develop democratic institutions abroad can also be seen in a number of other cases. Thus the movement toward elections in Honduras, Brazil, Peru, and Bolivia was linked to this administration, with the 1981 Honduran election in particular being described as one of the Carter administration's success stories.

Argentina, Chile, and Uruguay can be placed in the same category. Carter's role in the return to civilian government in Argentina was recognized in the enthusiastic reception he received when he visited that country after his departure from office; democratic factions in Chile perceived Carter as a friend and supporter; and, after Uruguay's 1984 election, the president-elect stated that "the vigorous policies of the Carter Administration were the most important outside influence on Uruguay's democratization process. . . . One of the few sources of significant support we had was the policy of the U.S. Government, which was constantly looking into human rights violations."[70]

A central feature of the Reagan administration's human rights policy was the belief that the cause of human rights could best be served by promoting democracy. This heavy emphasis on democratization as the primary tool for the implementing of a human rights policy inevitably exposed it to a particularly critical survey that exposed some flaws in efforts to promote democracy throughout the world.

One criticism concerned the administration's definition of "democracy," asserting that this term was being used in its most narrow sense to mean a system of periodic, competitive elections. According to this view, the administration was putting too high a value on formal democracy and on a process—elections—that in many of the world's nations could not be counted upon to ensure a truly democratic society.

A second major criticism alleged that the Reagan administration took actions that appeared to contradict its official commitment to the development of democracy abroad. These actions included the political and financial support given for much of its term of office, to such dictatorships as those of Marcos in the Philippines and Duvalier in Haiti. A similar contradiction was seen in the perceived too-soft treatment of the South African government and its policy of apartheid.

The Reagan administration's increasing investment in international military education and training programs (IMET) was identified as still another line of action running counter to its professed determination to bring more nations into the democratic camp. Critics denied the administration's claims that these programs would produce significant changes in the attitudes of trainees and their conduct when they returned home, saying that these claims were not consistent with what was known about the content of U.S. military training or the political behavior of Third World military establishments. Critics also maintained that the administration's IMET program was contributing to a more serious imbalance between the military and civilian components in Third World societies.

A final major criticism related to a program that the administration proposed and strongly promoted, the National Endowment for Democracy, established in 1983 as a private, nonpartisan, nonprofit organization, with access to U.S. Information Agency funds, to promote democratic values and institutions around the world. According to some critics, the endowment was being used in such less noble practices as entering internal political conflicts in other countries on a partisan basis. Examples cited were funds made available to the opponents of the Sandinista regime in Nicaragua and the financial support given to a French anti-Communist faction allegedly related to an extremist right-wing organization.

While the Reagan administration's performance in relation to its professed goal of promoting democracy abroad thus drew negative criticism, it also had some positive features. One point to its credit was the switch in administration policy vis-à-vis the Philippines. Departing from its policy of support for the repressive authoritarian regime of Filipino President Marcos, whom Vice-President Bush toasted in 1981 saying that "we love your adherence to democratic principles and democratic processes," the Reagan administration used its influence in 1986 to help bring the Marcos era to an end.

The Reagan administration's hand was also seen in the downfall of another right-wing dictator, Haiti's Jean-Claude Duvalier. Argentina and Guatemala are other examples of situations in which the administration's efforts produced results to which Human Rights Bureau head Elliott Abrams referred in commenting on "the widely noted success of the Reagan Administration in promoting human rights and democracy."[71]

SUMMARY

Tactics of both administrations for direct action on behalf of human rights involved, first, approaches to other governments through the use of both quiet and open diplomacy. Both administrations preferred to make their first representations through private channels, but were willing to go public with their concerns when doing so appeared to be necessary and/or useful. This pattern of action by both administrations contrasted with certain stereotypes relative to their human rights behavior: concerning Carter, that he neglected quiet diplomacy and was overly addicted to public condemnation of rights violators; and concerning Reagan, that his emphasis on quiet diplomacy constituted a break from the procedures of his predecessor and that he would eschew open censure of abusers.

The direct tactics employed by both administrations also included application of pressure and offering of inducements in order to alter the human rights performance of other governments. Carter's efforts to use U.S. aid programs for this purpose were hampered by resistance within the foreign service bureaucracy to attaching human rights conditions to aid programs, a problem that time and experience had largely resolved before Reagan came into office. A major form of the pressure/inducement tactic available to both administrations was U.S. action in international financial institutions, and both administrations took advantage of this influence channel. The two differed, however, in that the Reagan administration was more selective in the use of U.S. votes and influence to apply pressure on repressive regimes, dealing with them in a less evenhanded manner than did his predecessor.

Indirect tactics of the two administrations took two forms, the first of which was issuing annual reviews of the human rights practices of other governments, a legislatively mandated procedure. The two administrations followed substantially the same procedure in preparing these reports. In both cases, the reports were both commended as valuable contributions to a better understanding of human rights conditions around the world and censured for alleged omissions and distortions, which, according to critics, reflected certain political biases and/or purposes held by those who prepared the reports. The reports published by the two administrations differed at several points: (1) the material in the Carter reports included economic/social rights, a category that the Reagan administration rejected; and (2) the Reagan administration used the introductory section of the annual volumes to set forth its philosophy concerning human rights, a procedure that Carter did not follow.

The second indirect method used by both administrations for the implementation of their human rights policies was the promotion of democracy abroad, on the assumption that the existence of democratic institutions and practices provided the best protection for human rights. While both administrations operated on this thesis, democratization was given a heavier emphasis under Reagan than Carter and was a more explicit human rights policy tool for the former than for the latter.

NOTES

1. Patricia Derian, Milwaukee address, June 13, 1980.
2. U.S. Congress, House of Representatives, Committee on Foreign Affairs, *Human Rights and U.S. Foreign Policy: Hearings Before the Subcommittee on International Organizations*, 96th Cong., 2d Sess., May 2, 10; June 21; July 12; and August 2, 1979 (Washington, D.C.: U.S. Government Printing Office, 1979), p. 24.
3. Vassily Aksynov, "Overhaul U.S. Human Rights Policy?" *U.S. News and World Report*, March 2, 1981, p. 50.
4. U.S. Congress, House of Representatives, Committee on Foreign Affairs, *Review of U.S. Human Rights Policy: Hearings Before the Subcommittee on Human Rights and International Organizations*, 98th Cong., 1st Sess., March 3; June 28; and September 21, 1983 (Washington, D.C.: U.S. Government Printing Office, 1983), p. 89.
5. "MacNeil/Lehrer Report," Public Broadcasting System, February 10, 1981.
6. Conversation at the Department of State, October 1984.
7. Conversation at the Department of State, May 1985.
8. U.S. Congress, *Human Rights and U.S. Foreign Policy*, p. 349.
9. Conversation with Patricia Derian, September 1985.
10. Ibid.; Cynthia Brown, ed., *With Friends Like These*, The Americas Watch Report on Human Rights and U.S. Policy in Latin America (New York: Pantheon Books, 1985), p. 99.
11. Sources for the preceding discussion are Patricia Derian in U.S. Congress, House of Representatives, Committee on Foreign Affairs, *Human Rights in Asia: Non-Communist Countries: Hearings Before the Subcommittees on Asian and Pacific Affairs and on International Organizations*, 96th Cong., 2d Sess., February 4, 6, 7, 1980 (Washington, D.C.: U.S. Government Printing Office, 1980), p. 196; Cyrus R. Vance, *Hard Choices: Critical Years in America's Foreign Policy* (New York: Simon and Schuster, 1983), pp. 46, 317–319, 343; Zbigniew Brzezinski, *Power and Principle* (New York: Farrar, Straus, and Giroux, 1985), pp. 141, 154, 319, 407; and U.S. Congress, *Human Rights and U.S. Foreign Policy*, pp. 498, 501.
12. Vance, *Hard Choices*, p. 46.
13. U.S. Congress, *Human Rights and U.S. Foreign Policy*, pp. 17, 32–35.

14. Ibid, p. 498.

15. David Heaps, *Human Rights and U.S. Foreign Policy: The First Decade, 1973–1983* (New York: The American Association for the International Commission of Jurists, 1984), p. 16. (Hereafter cited as *Human Rights: The First Decade*).

16. Conversations at the State Department, October 1984.

17. U.S. Congress, *Human Rights and U.S. Foreign Policy*, p. 336.

18. U.S. Department of State, *Country Reports on Human Rights Practices for 1983: Report Submitted to the Committee on Foreign Affairs, House of Representatives and the Committee on Foreign Relations, the Senate* (Washington, D.C.: U.S. Government Printing Office, 1984), p. 4.

19. U.S. Congress, House of Representatives, Committee on Foreign Affairs, *The Phenomenon of Torture: Hearings and Markup Before the Subcommittee on Human Rights and International Organizations*, 98th Cong., 2d Sess., May 15 and 16 and September 6, 1984 (Washington, D.C.: U.S. Government Printing Office, 1984), pp. 211, 214.

20. Conversations at the State Department, May 1985.

21. U.S. Congress, House of Representatives, Committee on Foreign Affairs, *Political Killings by Governments of Their Citizens: Hearings Before the Subcommittee On Human Rights and International Organizations*, 98th Cong., 1st Sess., November 16 and 17, 1983 (Washington, D.C.: U.S. Government Printing Office, 1983), p. 214.

22. Americas Watch, Helsinki Watch, Lawyers Committee for International Human Rights, *Failure: the Reagan Administration's Human Rights Policy in 1983* (New York and Washington, D.C.: Authors, 1984), p. 52. (Hereafter cited as *Failure*).

23. U.S. Congress, *Political Killings*, p. 215.

24. U.S. Department of State, *Country Reports . . . for 1983*, p. 4.

25. Elliott Abrams, address at Georgetown University, October 1983.

26. U.S. Congress, House of Representatives, Committee on Foreign Affairs, *Religious Persecution of the Baha'is in Iran: Hearing Before the Subcommittee on Human Rights and International Organizations*, 98th Cong., 2nd Sess., May 2, 1984 (Washington, D.C.: U.S. Government Printing Office, 1984), pp. 23–24; George Shultz, address, Peoria, Illinois, February 22, 1984; *Failure*, p. 69; and conversations at the Department of State, October 1984.

27. U.S. Department of State, *Country Reports . . . for 1982*, pp. 10–11.

28. Elliott Abrams, in U.S. Congress, *The Phenomenon of Torture*, p. 173.

29. Elliott Abrams, address at Georgetown University, October 12, 1983.

30. *Failure*, pp. 20, 44, 70; Henry Gottlieb, "Romania Warned on Human Rights," *The Boston Globe*, December 16, 1985; and U.S. Congress, *Political Killings*, p. 214.

31. *Failure*, p. 75; U.S. Congress, *Religious Persecution*, p. 23; and Americas Watch, Helsinki Watch, Lawyers Committee for International Human Rights, *In the Face of Cruelty: The Reagan Administration's Human Rights in 1984* (New York and Washington, D.C.: Authors, 1985), pp. 66, 93.

32. David K. Shipler, "Reagan Tempers His View on Soviets," *The New York Times*, December 11, 1985.

33. *In the Face of Cruelty*, p. 62.

34. Brown, *With Friends Like These*, p. 132.

35. Shultz, address, Peoria.

36. Ibid.

37. *In the Face of Cruelty*, p. 114; *Failure*, p. 102; Lawyers Committee for Human Rights, the Watch Committees, *The Reagan Administration's Record on Human Rights*

in 1985 (New York and Washington, D.C.: Author, 1986), pp. 25–26; U.S. Congress, *Religious Persecution*, pp. 9, 22.

38. *Failure*, pp. 102–103.

39. Lawyers Committee, *The Reagan Administration's Record*, p. 29.

40. W. Frick Curry and Joanne Royce, *Enforcing Human Rights: Congress and the Multilateral Banks*, International Policy Report (Washington, D.C.: Center for International Policy, 1985), p. 8.

41. Caleb Rossiter, *The Financial Hit List*, International Policy Report (Washington, D.C.: Center for International Policy, 1984), p. 5.

42. Patricia Derian, in U.S. Congress, *Human Rights in Asia: Non-Communist Countries*, p. 183.

43. Michael Armacost, in U.S. Congress, *Human Rights in Asia: Non-Communist Countries*, pp. 191, 192.

44. Charles W. Freeman, in U.S. Congress, *Human Rights in Asia: Communist Countries*, p. 48.

45. U.S. Congress, *Human Rights and U.S. Foreign Policy, p. 19.*

46. Ibid., pp. 39, 330, 336; U.S. Congress, *Human Rights in Asia: Non-Communist Countries*, p. 192; Richard E. Feinberg, *U.S. Human Policy: Latin America*, International Policy Report (Washington, D.C.: Center for International Policy, 1980), pp. 2–3.

47. Tom Farer, in U.S. Congress, *Political Killings*, p. 212.

48. Tom Farer, in U.S. Congress, *Human Rights and U.S. Foreign Policy*, p. 63; Stephen B. Cohen, "Conditioning U.S. Security Assistance on Human Rights Practices," *American Journal of International Law* (January–April 1982): 264.

49. Caleb Rossiter, *Human Rights: The Carter Record, the Regan Reaction*, International Policy Report (Washington, D.C.: Center for International Policy, 1984), pp. 7–10 (hereafter cited as *Carter Record, Reagan Reaction*).

50. Ibid., pp. 8, 11.

51. Curry and Royce, *Enforcing Human Rights*, pp. 8, 9.

52. For the Carter record on votes in IFIs, see U.S. Congress, *Human Rights and U.S. Foreign Policy*, pp. 324–329; *Carter Record, Reagan Reaction*, pp. 8, 11–19; and Curry and Royce, *Enforcing Human Rights*, p. 14. For an analysis of the role of IFIs in human rights programs, see Curry and Royce, *Enforcing Human Rights*.

53. Curry and Royce, *Enforcing Human Rights*, p. 10.

54. Ibid.

55. *Carter Record, Reagan Reaction*, p. 18.

56. Abrams' comments were included in his Georgetown University address, October 12, 1983; in U.S. Congress, *The Phenomenon of Torture*, p. 155; and in U.S. Congress, *Religious Persecution*, p. 23.

57. "The MacNeil/Lehrer Report," February 10, 1981.

58. Shirley Christian, "Anti-Sandinistas Vow to Cut Abuses," *The New York Times*, August 24, 1985.

59. *Carter Record, Reagan Reaction*, p. 25.

60. Stephen Bosworth, in Curry and Royce, *Enforcing Human Rights*, p. 12.

61. Jim Leach, in U.S. Congress, House of Representatives, Committee on Banking, Finance, and Urban Affairs, *Proposed U.S. Participation in the Inter-American Investment Corporation: Hearing Before the Subcommittee on International Development*

Institutions and Finance, 98th Congress, 2nd Session, August 1, 1984 (Washington, D.C.: U.S. Government Printing Office, 1984), p. 36.

62. Ibid., pp. 23, 24.

63. U.S. Congress, House of Representatives, Committee on Foreign Affairs, Committee on Banking, Finance, and Urban Affairs, and the Subcommittee on Africa, *Human Rights Policies at the Multilateral Development Banks: Joint Hearing Before the Subcommittee on International Development Institutions and Finance*, 98th Cong., 1st Sess., June 22, 1983 (Washington, D.C.: U.S. Government Printing Office, 1983), p. 15. For the Reagan Administration's record and attitude toward the use of IFIs, see also Curry and Royce, *Enforcing Human Rights*, pp. 14, 17, 18; *Carter Record, Reagan Reaction*, pp. 14–17; and *The Reagan Administration's Record*, p. 9.

64. Conversations at the Department of State, October 1984, and U.S. Congress, *Review of U.S. Human Rights Policy*, p. 71.

65. U.S. Congress, *Human Rights in Asia: Non-Communist Countries*, pp. 177, 186, 187.

66. U.S. Congress, *Human Rights and U.S. Foreign Policy*, pp. 360, 387.

67. Conversations at the Department of State, October 1984.

68. U.S. Congress, *Review of U.S. Human Rights Policy*, p. 35. See also Ibid., pp. 4, 55, 59, 60, 71, 104; and U.S. Department of State, *Country Reports . . . for 1982*, p. 13.

69. U.S. Congress, *Human Rights and U.S. Foreign Policy*, p. 20.

70. International Human Rights Law Group and Washington Office on Latin America, *From Shadow into Sunlight: A Report on the 1984 Uruguayan Electoral Process* (Washington, D.C.: Authors, 1985), p. 38. For discussions on Carter and democracy, see U.S. Department of State, *Country Reports . . . for 1979*, p. 4; Brzezinski, *Power and Principle*, p. 55; Feinberg, *U.S. Human Rights Policy: Latin America*, pp. 2, 8–10; U.S. Congress, *Human Rights in Asia: Non-Communist Countries*, p. 183; and Brown, *With Friends Like These*, p. 22. Conversations at the Department of State, October 1984 and September 1985 also contributed material for this discussion.

71. The bases for the preceding discussion are U.S. Department of State, *Country Reports . . . for 1982*, p. 8; Reagan address to the British Parliament, June 8, 1982; Shultz, Peoria Address, February 22, 1984; conversations at the Department of State, October 1984; U.S. Congress, *The Phenomenon of Torture*, pp. 153, 156; Letters to the Editor, and Anthony Lewis, "Why We Celebrate," *The New York Times*, January 10 and February 27, 1986; William Shannon, "Promoting Democracy," *The Boston Globe*, December 11, 1985; Michael Putzel, "Reagan Shines in Dictators' Fall," *The Centre Daily Times*, State College, Pa., March 2, 1986; publications of the National Endowment for Democracy, Washington, D.C.; Brown, *With Friends Like These*, pp. 9, 89, 91; Sidney Blumenthal, "U.S. Endowment Funds Anti-Sandinista Group," *The Washington Post*, March 19, 1986; and *Failure*, p. 28. See also J. Samuel Fitch, *Human Rights and U.S. Military Aid Programs* (Washington, D.C.: Washington Office on Latin America, 1985).

5

Carter, Reagan, and Human Rights in South Africa and South Korea

This chapter compares the human rights policies of the Carter and Reagan administrations by looking at these policies as they related to the human rights situations in South Africa and South Korea.

SOUTH AFRICA

The Republic of South Africa has a population of 32,112,000 of which 73 percent are black, 15 percent are white, 9 percent are coloured (racially mixed), and 3 percent are Asians, mostly Indian. The country is governed under a constitution adopted in 1984 that provides for a strong executive state president, chosen by an electoral College consisting of representatives of the three chambers of Parliament.

The parliamentary chambers are constituted on a racial basis, with separate houses for whites, coloureds, and Indians. Of these three, the first, or white, is dominant in that it controls the election of the president who, in turn, can veto legislation, declare war, and summon/dismiss Parliament. The only form of political participation permitted to blacks is the privilege of voting for the unicameral legislatures in the ten Bantustans, created to serve as the obligatory homelands of those blacks who are not considered to be needed in the segregated labor system.

The contrast in the positions of whites and blacks also appears in other aspects of South African national society. The life expectancy of whites is 70 years, that of blacks, 57.5; the infant mortality rate for blacks is 94 per 1,000, for whites, 15; whites have a 98 percent literacy rate, blacks, 50; the average annual earnings of white workers is $8,260, that of black workers, $1,815; the average monthly pension payment for whites is $94, for blacks, $41; and, while the government's per capita spending for the education of whites is $780, the expenditure for blacks is only $110. Finally, while the

Bantustans have been described as "barren reserves," the white-controlled land contains the country's most fertile land, cities, and rich mineral deposits.[1]

For the purposes of this book the most significant feature of the South African profile is its system of racial segregation, called apartheid. Rooted in the social attitudes of the early European settlers in this area, who considered African customs to be barbaric, apartheid took two forms: petty and grand. Petty apartheid, which has become less strict as a result of reforms, called for racial separation in lavatories, restaurants, railway cars, buses, swimming pools, and other public facilities. Grand apartheid involved the system of racially biased laws that restricted the movement of blacks and denied them a share in the political process.

South Africa's apartheid system has long been the object of censure from the world community, occupying a continuous place on the agenda of the United Nations General Assembly since its first session in 1946. The assembly's attempts to bring an end to this system have included such actions as the 1962 resolution calling on all UN members to break diplomatic relations with South Africa and to take other steps, including cessation of trade with this nation, and the adoption in 1973 of a Convention on the Suppression and Punishment of the Crime of Apartheid, which, as of 1983, had seventy-three parties and six signators (not including the United States). Further evidence of broad disapproval of South Africa's system of apartheid is the action that the foreign ministers of eleven of the twelve European Community (Common Market) countries took in 1985, imposing an embargo on oil, arms, and law-enforcement equipment, a ban on military and nuclear cooperation, and discouragement of cultural and scientific links.

The United States and South Africa have long been bound by close political and economic ties. Twenty percent of South Africa's total foreign capital is provided by some 350 U.S. companies, functioning in areas that are highly important to the republic, such as computers and automobiles. As of 1984, the total U.S. financial investment in South Africa was $15 billion. The same year the United States was the republic's principal trading partner, with the United States buying base metals and mineral products and selling machinery and corn. South Africa provides the United States with a number of strategic minerals: from 1980 to 1983 61 percent of its cobalt, 55 percent of its chromium, 49 percent of its platinum, 44 percent of its vanadium, and 39 percent of its manganese. South Africa's geographic position in relation to seaways adds to its strategic importance, as does its role in dealing with such southern African problems as the leftist regime in Angola and independence, in fact, for Namibia.[2]

South Africa's importance to the United States has combined with its system of apartheid to pose a critical and difficult problem for America's foreign policy makers, who have struggled to find a way to retain South Africa as an ally and yet demonstrate U.S. opposition to apartheid. According to

Kevin Danaher, the United States could deal with this problem in any one of three ways: friendly relations, symbolic pressure, or material pressure, with the last being the only one that has not been tried.

The Nixon and Reagan Administrations implemented friendly relations with the apartheid regime and conditions grew worse for the black majority. The Carter Administration tried verbal and symbolic pressure but Pretoria shrugged off the criticism and cracked down even harder on its black opposition.[3]

The reaction of the Carter and Reagan administrations to apartheid in South Africa, to which Danaher briefly alludes, will be the focus of the following discussion. Apartheid in South Africa thus provides a specific situation in which the human rights policies of the two administrations can be compared. In this comparison attention will center on those actions that could be considered as working against apartheid and thus promoting the cause of human rights and those actions, or failures to act, that could be considered as working in the opposite direction.

The Carter Administration

The Carter administration's response to the problem of human rights in the Republic of South Africa was an official commitment to seek an end to the policy of apartheid, with this change to be brought about through peaceful, nonviolent methods.

While the administration's objective could be clearly stated, a number of complicating factors hindered its implementation. Among these complications was the relationship between the situation and developments in South Africa and those of other African states where blacks were struggling to end white domination. This movement for black liberation was, however, only one part of the political scene in southern Africa in the 1970s. Another critical part was the East-West conflict.

The intermingling of these two elements in African politics produced at least two results. First, Black Africans were unsure what they could really expect from the United States by way of support for their cause. Black militants in southern Africa strongly suspected that whatever the United States did in this region, it would do only for cold war reasons. Applied to South Africa, this line of thinking produced the conclusion that U.S. policy toward the republic would be guided by American—and Western—strategic interests that in turn required a strong South Africa protected by black client states dependent on the republic's political, economic, and military support. U.S. support for the white regime in South Africa was an implied corollary of this thesis.[4]

A second result of the intermingling of the black liberation and cold war elements in the African political picture was a Carter administration policy that attempted to satisfy the demands of both. As Carter's secretary of state, Cyrus Vance, has noted:

We recognized that identifying the United States with the cause of majority rule was the best way to prevent Soviet and Cuban exploitation of the racial conflicts of southern Africa. But our decision to break sharply with the policy of the past did not merely reflect concern about Soviet influence or revolutionary movements. We were committed to majority rule, self-determination, and racial equality as a matter of fairness and basic human rights. If the United States did not support social and political justice in Rhodesia, Namibia, and South Africa itself, Africans would correctly dismiss our human rights policies as mere cold war propaganda, employed at the expense of the peoples of Africa.[5]

For the Carter administration, dismantling apartheid in South Africa was thus both a policy end and a policy means. It was an end in the sense that apartheid was seen as a denial of the human rights of the black majority in this country, and therefore a situation whose termination was a worthy objective in itself; and it was a means in the sense that a U.S. commitment to seek an end to apartheid would serve American interests by providing an effective counterweight to Soviet and other leftist influence in southern Africa.

The Carter administration's attempt to bring the anti-apartheid and anticommunism threads of its African foreign policy together had a parallel in another policy problem: the balancing of the human rights imperative, calling for an end to apartheid in South Africa, on one hand, and, on the other, the felt need to enlist this country's support in U.S. efforts to deal with other regional problems. The significance of the latter point lies in the fact that, as the strongest state economically and politically in southern Africa, the republic could exert considerable influence on the direction of regional affairs. The Carter administration was well aware of the positive contribution South Africa could make to resolving regional problems and demonstrated this awareness, for example, in its reaction to three resolutions introduced in the UN Security Council in the fall of 1977. These African-sponsored resolutions called for the imposition of punitive sanctions against South Africa, and, in view of the declared American opposition to apartheid, would presumably have enjoyed U.S. support. As Carter's national security advisor Zbigniew Brzezinski acknowledged, however, a "major constraint on U.S. policy lay precisely in the fact that the United States looked to South Africa to assist in procuring a Rhodesian settlement."[6]

Conscious as it was of such political realities as the need for South Africa's cooperation in dealing with regional issues, the Carter administration could not ignore another reality: South Africa was, itself, a major contributor to regional instability because of its system of racial segregation. Because of this fact of African life, the administration could not retreat from its commitment to seek an end to apartheid in the Republic of South Africa.

All these above considerations must be taken into account in reviewing and evaluating what the Carter administration did and did not do in regard to apartheid in South Africa. The presence of policy imperatives that were not always mutually reinforcing could not help but produce actions that lacked consistency, at least on the surface. This problem of consistency also affected another Carter postulate concerning apartheid in South Africa: that the desired move away from apartheid should be peaceful. This position was qualified, however, by a realization that, if the white regime in South Africa continued to refuse to abandon apartheid, this country's oppressed black majority could not be expected to reject violent methods forever. In the words of Carter's leading expert on southern African affairs, Anthony Lake, quoting John F. Kennedy, "those who make peaceful evolution impossible will make violent revolution inevitable."[7]

In view of all the complicating factors in the social and political scene in southern Africa, it is not surprising that the Carter administration's efforts to implement its anti-apartheid policy did not always produce results that could be seen as helping the cause of human rights in South Africa. As one African specialist in this administration conceded: "In the heavy diplomatic slogging over Rhodesia and Namibia, we let up on internal reform in South Africa. I can understand why people say we went easy on them."[8] The feeling that the Carter administration failed to exert significant pressure on South Africa was bolstered by such actions as the negative votes cast by the United States on a series of proposals put forward in the thirty-third session of the UN General Assembly. One of these proposals called for an end to all collaboration with South Africa in the nuclear field. Another sought an end to all economic collaboration with South Africa, asking the Security Council to consider economic sanctions against the republic, and called for such other measures as the termination of the activities of banks, the International Monetary Fund, and other sources of credit in South Africa and the denial of ship and air facilities for travel involving this country. A third, dealing with military collaboration with South Africa, requested the Security Council to declare all military or nuclear collaboration with South Africa to be a threat to international peace and security, and asked the council to take mandatory measures to end all military and nuclear collaboration with South Africa and supplies of materials and technology to it. All three proposals were adopted by overwhelming majorities.[9]

The alleged failure of the Carter administration to use situations like these UN votes as pressure devices vis-à-vis South Africa could be explained, as suggested above, by the perceived necessity to assign a higher priority to U.S. policy objectives in other areas of southern Africa. Another possible explanation could be found in a thesis presented by National Security Advisor Brzezinski in his December 1977 U.S.–South African policy outline: "Our influence and leverage within South Africa are limited. We do not have the capacity to greatly influence events from afar according to our will."[10]

A critic of the Carter administration would probably reply that if, as one

Carter official said, South Africa's internal policies were always seen as "the toughest nut to crack," the reason could be that the administration erred in its choice of tactics for dealing with the South African regime. "The greatest single failure of the Carter Administration," according to one critic, "was its political, ideological inability, and unwillingness, to recognize that there had been improvements in South Africa." For example, when the South African government took such steps as permitting integration in Catholic schools and at certain levels of athletic competition, there was no commendatory response from Washington. Experiences like these were seen as helping to create a South African perception that the Carter administration was given only to criticism, with no countervailing expressions of approval or appreciation for progress away from apartheid. This perception was blamed for the administration's declining influence with the South African regime.[11]

The record of the Carter administration's efforts to serve the cause of human rights in South Africa by opposing apartheid thus has its negative aspects. This record, however, also contains evidence of positive action taken to implement its anti-apartheid policy. Thus, while the administration cast some negative votes in the UN General Assembly on resolutions concerning the situation in South Africa, it also used the debates on these resolutions to declare publicly its opposition to racial segregation in that country. In a November 22, 1978, assembly meeting, for example, the U.S. representative stated:

The U.S. Government has made our view clear to the Government of South Africa, has stressed our commitment to human rights, and has called for the elimination of apartheid and the full political participation of all South Africans on an equal basis. . . . We don't expect these changes to occur overnight, but have stated that without evident progress in this direction our relations with South Africa will deteriorate.

The American representative included in his remarks a reference to President Carter's State of the Union address, in which he also asserted that U.S.–South African relations would suffer if the latter failed to begin a "progressive transformation toward full political participation for all people." After declaring that the aim of the United States was not confrontation but achievement of progressive change, the U.S. delegate quoted the comments of Secretary of State Cyrus Vance:

Our policy toward South Africa should not be misunderstood. We have no wish to see whites driven from the home of their forefathers, [but] suggest only that they seek a way to live in peace and justice with the majority of their fellow citizens. South Africans of all races . . . should decide their country's future. We do not wish to impose a timetable or a blueprint for this progress. . . . But I hope that the beginning of basic progress will soon be seen.

The American representative concluded his remarks by stating that we are watching events in South Africa closely for signs of change... [and] we are actively trying to influence and persuade South Africa to change its policies.[12]

This effort to influence and persuade was also carried on in private, direct talks with South African leaders, like Vice-President Walter Mondale's 1977 meeting in Vienna with Prime Minister Balthazar J. Vorster. This meeting was an example of what Security Advisor Brzezinski referred to as President Carter's preference for the "direct approach." Vice-President Mondale used it to assure the prime minister that future U.S.–South African relations would depend on Pretoria's attitude toward political and racial change in southern Africa, including the beginning of a progressive transformation of South African society away from apartheid.

In his conversation with the prime minister, Mondale also stressed the fact that the American policy was rooted in the administration's view of human rights and was not simply an expression of its anticommunism. He assured Vorster that the United States wanted good relations with South Africa and was prepared to work closely with this country. However, he added a warning that if South Africa failed to concern itself seriously with the political and racial injustices of Rhodesia, Namibia, and South Africa, the United States would be compelled to abandon its opposition to mandatory international sanctions against South Africa. In presenting his administration's policy for southern Africa, Vice-President Mondale did not, as Prime Minister Vorster claimed, assert that this policy included a demand that South Africa adopt the "one man, one vote" rule for political participation. This, according to Secretary of State Cyrus Vance, "was not what Fritz said." By making this statement, Secretary Vance refuted the charge that Mondale had committed a "blunder that killed our relations with South Africa."[13]

Through both public and private channels, then, the Carter administration sought to fulfill the policy goal it set in 1977, "to keep up the pressure so that by 1980 there would be marked progress in dismantling apartheid in South Africa."[14] The pressure, in fact, was sufficiently strong to lead a member of the Reagan administration to describe the approach of the two administrations to the South African government in terms of "bad cop, good cop." Carter, in this official's opinion, was the "bad cop," the hard one who "got their attention," and "scared them by showing them that there was much opposition in the United States to the way things were done" in South Africa. While the Reagan administration regularly condemned the South African regime for such actions as police sweeps through black communities, Carter, faced with this kind of situation, "would have been tougher."[15] This perception of Carter, apparently also held by black leaders in South Africa, helps to explain Carter's popularity with this segment of South African society.

One factor that helped produce this image of Carter as the tough opponent of apartheid was the outspokenness, which, according to some observers, was more characteristic of the first half of his term of office than it was of the second. Those who assert that there was a change in the administration's tactics away from frequent public statements condemning Pretoria's racial policies have different explanations for this alleged switch. Thus Chester A. Crocker, writing as a Georgetown University academician, asserted that the "verbal flagellation and lectures from the American pulpit" had been abandoned because they were counterproductive. This opinion was shared by a State Department official who saw the Carter administration as realizing that public censure of the South African government was producing more resentment than willingness to change, a realization that led to a change in tactics.

If indeed there was a change in the Carter administration's tactics for dealing with apartheid, the reason may also have been developments within the administration in regard to policy priorities. The administration may have become less inclined to make frequent and strong public attacks on apartheid in South Africa because other policy concerns were pushing human rights off the center of the foreign policy stage. This thesis, that a change occurred in the administration's perspective, was advanced, for example, by Kevin Danaher, who has contended that a policy debate within the administration was ultimately won by the "globalists," whose emphasis on the East-West struggle had the effect of reducing local issues, such as apartheid, to a place of secondary importance.[16]

The Reagan Administration

As noted, it has been contended that the "globalist" outlook dominated the Carter administration's approach to South African affairs late in its term in office, with the result that the administration came to view the U.S.–South African relationship within the context of the East-West struggle. This, however, was not the way the Reagan administration's transition team saw the preceding administration as this State Department group proceeded with its work of preparing for Reagan's entry into the presidency. One of the products of the team's labors was an African policy paper that, among other things, asserted that the Carter administration suffered from "a severe case of regionalitis": paying too much attention to African affairs and not enough to the need to deal with Soviet influence on the continent.

This appraisal of the Carter administration is debatable, but the main thrust of the Reagan administration's policy toward Africa in general and South Africa in particular is certain. This orientation was revealed in one administration policy document dealing with a meeting involving Chester Crocker and some South African leaders, during which Crocker "stressed that top U.S. priority is to stop Soviet encroachment in Africa." In another confidential memo, discussion centered on the perception, shared by South African leaders and the Reagan administration, that "the chief threat to the realization . . . of stability and cooperation in the region . . . is the presence and influence of the Soviet Union and its allies."[17]

The Reagan administration's heavy emphasis on anticommunism explains much about its approach to the problem of human rights in South Africa, since this constituted one of the reasons for the administration's determination to maintain friendly relations with Pretoria. This determination, in turn, helps to explain the administration's consistent adherence to the tactic of constructive engagement, which it believed to be the most effective way to achieve the expressed goal of encouraging peaceful change away from apartheid in South Africa.

Under Secretary of State for Political Affairs Lawrence S. Eagleburger described this objective in an address on "Southern Africa: America's Responsibility for Peace and Change" on June 23, 1983. The speech has been described as "the result of intense work within the bureaucracy" and "the Bible on its subject." In the section on South Africa, Secretary Eagleburger stated:

It is essential that South Africans get on with the business of deciding and shaping their own future. The political system in South Africa is morally wrong. We stand against injustice, and, therefore, we must reject the legal and political premises and consequences of apartheid. . . .

"The domestic racial system in South Africa will change," continued Eagleburger, and, consequently, the administration's policy was directed "not at whether a nonracial order is in South Africa's future or what the shape of that nonracial order will be, but at how it will be arrived at." In his words, "a peaceful change depends on support from those who reject, as we do, both alignment with the current racial order and violence as a means of ending it." The administration's policy of constructive engagement was obviously designed to bring American support for the kind of change that Eagleburger described, a change that he saw to be already under way.[18]

These, then, were the premises for the Reagan administration's tactic of practicing constructive engagement in the effort to rid South Africa of apartheid: a belief in the need for change, rejection of violence as a means to this end, and a conviction that the current elements in the South African scene, including the country's white leadership, were already working toward the desired change. The tactical conclusion from all this, then, was that the proper procedure for the United States was "to concentrate on positive steps which back constructive change and those who are working for it."

The "positive steps" to which Eagleburger referred included support for trade unionists, students, entrepreneurs, government leaders, cultural-political movements, civic associations, and religious organizations that "through their commitment to peaceful change away from apartheid, can help make a better future for all citizens of South Africa." As evidence of the administration's resolve to provide tangible support for the constructive elements in South African society, Eagleburger then cited a number of programs that the Reagan administration initiated in its first two years in office, including:

1. A $4 million-a-year scholarship program for some one hundred black South African students for study in the United States.
2. In cooperation with the AFL-CIO, training for South African labor leaders, to improve the collective bargaining ability of black and mixed trade unions.
3. In cooperation with the National African Federated Chamber of Commerce of South Africa, support for small business development in the black community.
4. A tutorial program to assist black high school students to prepare for the matriculation exams serving as preludes to professional careers.

In keeping with what it considered to be a positive approach to South Africa, leading to these programs, the Reagan administration rejected the use of such pressure tactics as sanctions to induce more rapid change in South Africa. In the opinion of the administration, such pressure was not needed; as Secretary of State Shultz declared in 1985, South Africa's white government "has already crossed a historical divide" in the reform of its racial policies, and "South Africa is changing for the better." Chester Crocker, who has been credited with the authorship of the policy of constructive engagement, agreed, saying that "the process of change away from apartheid has begun. . . . It is being dismantled."[19]

The progress that was perceived to be already under way was one reason for the rejection of sanctions against South Africa beyond those already in place through congressional action: an arms embargo and restrictions on the sale of equipment to South Africa's military, police, and other agencies enforcing apartheid. In Crocker's words, "we have no intention of waging economic warfare on South Africa and its people";[20] to do so, through punitive economic sanctions, was inappropriate not only because Pretoria was already moving in the right direction, but because it would work an economic hardship on the people whose interests were presumably at the heart of the anti-apartheid movement. Moreover, in the administration's opinion, sanctions would not really influence the pace and direction of change—a reflection of its belief that the United States actually had little power to influence events in South Africa.

The Reagan administration's policy of constructive engagement was reaffirmed in late 1985, in spite of what some observers felt to be a worsening of the situation in South Africa and a rising tide of criticism of this approach to the white rulers of South Africa. According to the American ambassador to South Africa, Herman Nickel, this confirmation followed an extensive policy review at the highest administration levels; in his words, "we haven't heard a better alternative to the approach we've been taking." The United

States would thus continue to seek a friendly relationship with South Africa with "an emphasis on the positive."[21]

The Reagan administration was convinced that, in adhering to its policy of constructive engagement, it was lending positive support to the cause of human rights in South Africa, since, in its opinion, this policy held the greatest promise of inducing the white regime to abandon apartheid. The programs undertaken on behalf of black students, labor leaders, and others were also viewed as contributing to the alleviating of some of the economic and social injustices resulting from apartheid.

In what could be seen as another effort to serve the cause of human rights in South Africa, Reagan retreated somewhat from his resistance to sanctions against the South African government by issuing an executive order containing a set of measures "aimed at the machinery of apartheid." This order, delivered in September 1985, included these provisions:

1. A ban on all computer exports to military, police, and security forces and agencies involved in the enforcement of apartheid.

2. A ban on loans to the South African government except those designed to improve economic opportunities, or educational, housing, and health facilities open and accessible to all South Africans.

3. A prohibition on nuclear technology exports unless the material was required to oversee nuclear nonproliferation or for humanitarian purposes.

4. A possible ban on U.S. imports of Krugerrands (South African gold coins).

5. A worldwide ban on U.S. government assistance to any company employing more than twenty-five people in South Africa that did not adhere to what the U.S. considers to be fair and nondiscriminatory employment practices.[22]

This presidential action was seen not only as an abandonment of the long-standing opposition to sanctions, but as a reversal of the equally long-standing policy of constructive engagement. Moreover, in the opinion of news columnist David B. Ottaway, Reagan's adoption of punitive measures against South Africa "placed the pursuit of reform inside [South Africa] at the top of the U.S. agenda in dealing with southern Africa, rather than concentrating U.S. efforts on South Africa's relations with its neighbors." A somewhat contrary view was expressed by U.S. Ambassador Nickel, who said that the decision to impose sanctions did not contradict his government's policy of using diplomatic persuasion to dismantle apartheid.[23]

President Reagan's imposition of sanctions reflected what appeared to be a growing impatience over the failure of the white government of South Africa to move more decisively and rapidly to end apartheid and an increasing willingness on the part of the administration to put pressure on Pretoria. Evidence that the Reagan administration was becoming less tolerant of the pace of change in South Afric began to appear late in 1984, when the administration was reported to be warning Pretoria that its continued repression of blacks could have both "internal and international costs." This warning, described as "some of the most harsh criticism ever directed to the South African Government by the Reagan Administration," came on the heels of a raid on several black townships, one of the most extensive security operations to be conducted since the Soweto riots of 1976. The declaration of a state of emergency by South African President P. W. Botha in July 1985 evoked another critical comment from the Reagan administration, asserting that apartheid was "largely responsible for the violence in South Africa."

This combination of increasing levels of violence in South Africa and of American criticism of Pretoria's handling of its internal affairs produced a decided strain in U.S.–South African relations. Secretary of State George Shultz acknowledged this condition but repeated his administration's belief that true peace would come to South Africa only when apartheid ended. The secretary also conceded that the policy of using quiet diplomacy ("constructive engagement") to move South Africa away from apartheid was "very controversial," but he rejected alternative approaches that, in his opinion, would have the effect of putting distance between the United States and South Africa and thereby reducing American leverage and influence with Pretoria. The administration coupled its defense of its policy of constructive engagement with a reiteration of its opposition to such tactics as the action taken by France, which suspended new investment in South Africa, a step that the administration said could "undermine South Africa's economy and create additional hardships for black South Africans."[24]

Despite the strain in U.S.–South African relations that followed from the heavier volume of critical comments, the Reagan administration continued to escalate its pressure on Pretoria. In late July 1985, for example, the administration called on the South African government to lift its emergency decree. This initiative, labeled "the strongest American statement"[25] to be issued since the state of emergency was declared, was taken at a time of increasing pressure from Congress for American action in regard to the situation in South Africa, and when the UN Security Council was debating sanctions against the country.

At the same time that it was calling for an end to the emergency decree, the Reagan administration was urging that talks be held between the white regime in South Africa and the leadership of the black community and criticizing President Botha for his refusal to meet with the black leader, Bishop Desmond M. Tutu. These actions exemplified the increasing withdrawal by the Reagan administration from its reliance on the quiet diplomacy of constructive engagement. In a public statement in August the Reagan administration urged the South African government to make "bold decisions" to end racial violence and give "political rights, justice, and equality" to South Africa's black majority.

While public statements on the racial situation in South Africa were appearing in increasing numbers, the tactic of private diplomacy was not being neglected. In August 1985, for example, Reagan's national security advisor Robert C. McFarlane met representatives of the South African government, including its foreign minister, in Vienna to urge them to make changes in their government's racial policies and to warn them that an emotional climate in the United States could lead to a harder U.S. policy toward South Africa.

In 1985, both in public statements and private conversations, the Reagan administration became more specific in its representations to South Africa on the subject of apartheid and what should be done to eliminate it. The administration stated its belief that the outlawed African National Congress should be allowed to participate in discussions with the white leadership concerning the future of South Africa and that one of the congress's main leaders, Nelson Mandela, should be released from prison; that Pretoria should establish institutions that would enable blacks to make formal complaints concerning brutality and other forms of misbehavior attributed to South Africa's security forces, and to do so without fear of harassment; and protested the arrest of Nelson Mandela's wife, Winnie.

Late 1985 and early 1986 saw other indications of a more aggressive stand by the Reagan administration against apartheid and an increased willingness to press the South African government to end it. When U.S. Ambassador Herman Nickel returned to Johannesburg in September 1985, after having been recalled to Washington three months earlier, he called on the South African government to move beyond "mere statements" and to begin dismantling "key features" of apartheid.[26] At about the same time, Assistant Secretary of State for African Affairs Chester A. Crocker described as "not adequate" the changes in South African policy[27] recently announced by the white South African leadership, and in December President Reagan's Human Rights Day commemorative remarks contained the harshest criticism he had ever made of the South African regime. Using this occasion to assert that the state of emergency decreed by Pretoria had become a license for the police to silence critics and curtail the most basic civil liberties of black citizens, he also declared that apartheid was inhuman and abhorrent, and that "it is time the Government of South Africa took steps to end it and to reach out for compromise and reconciliation to end the turmoil in that strife-torn land."[28]

In another departure from the previous Reagan administration approach to the human rights situation in South Africa, Assistant Secretary of State Crocker, on a January 1986 visit to South Africa, altered the pattern of previous visits by touring two segregated townships, reversing his practice of meeting only with leaders of the white regime. Crocker's conduct on this visit assumes greater significance when viewed against the background of the feeling, prevalent among black South Africans, that the Reagan administration was hostile to them.

It is thus apparent that the Reagan administration's approach to the human rights situation in South Africa underwent significant changes in the later years of its term of office. Departing from previous administration policy, at least formally, the president issued his executive order imposing sanctions on the South African government. The significance of this action as evidence of a changed Reagan attitude was considerably lessened, however, by the fact that the order was the product of pressures on the president rather than his freely taken initiative. These pressures came from different directions, foremost of which was the very real possibility that Congress would enact legislation imposing sanctions on South Africa that the president opposed and threatened to veto. Moreover, there was support within the president's own party for congressionally enacted sanctions. Some of this support came from what has been described as a new generation of conservative Republicans who argued that there was no political future for them in being seen as defenders of the government of South Africa. The strength of the movement for legislated sanctions confronted the president with the likelihood of losing control over U.S. policy vis-à-vis South Africa and suffering a humiliating political defeat. The response to these possibilities was the executive order. While this presidential step represented a kind of pressure on South Africa that the administration had long opposed, its terms were milder than those contained in the legislation pending in Congress. The latter would have left room for stronger action in a year if one of eight conditions set forth in the legislation had not been met by South Africa, a provision absent from the executive order. Again, while the order banned bank loans to South Africa's public sector, it exempted loans that would "improve the welfare or economic opportunities of persons disadvantaged by apartheid," a provision that opened the door to U.S. bank loans to segregated townships, homelands, and other features of apartheid. And, as a final example of the weakness of the order as compared with proposed congressional sanctions, the latter would have applied to *all* nuclear exports to Pretoria until South Africa signed the Nuclear Non-Proliferation Treaty, whereas the order permitted transfer of nuclear technology and expertise if the secretary of state determined that such exports were "necessary for humanitarian reasons to protect the public health and safety."

While the movement for sanctions was gaining strength, so was the criticism of the administration's policy of constructive engagement. One critic, Representative William H. Gray, III, speaking in August 1985, asserted that since this policy was adopted, "what you see is that oppression has gotten worse. . . . We can't point to one thing that has actually changed in the past four and a half years. Namibia is still occupied, oppression continues, and we've seen over six hundred people killed in recent months."

Other critics called constructive engagement a policy "without teeth," one creating the impression that the administration was "pro-Pretoria," and based on an assumption that proved to be invalid: that South Africa was really interested in the "carrot" of good relations with the United States. Moreover, the allegation was made that the administration itself had given evidence that it believed the policy to have serious shortcomings by adopting measures that ran counter to it: presidential signature to a bill banning the sale of computers to South African police, the recall of this country's ambassador to South Africa after South Africa's raids into Botswana and Angola, and increasingly loud condemnations of apartheid by administration spokespersons.[29]

In its adoption late in its tenure in office of a sterner approach to the South African regime, the Reagan administration faced a credibility problem growing out of years of actions toward this regime that created the impression that it was more pro-Pretoria than it was anti-apartheid. The problem dated from the administration's first year in office, when, in explaining the administration's policy of constructive engagement in South Africa, Assistant Secretary of State for African Affairs Chester Crocker declared, "It does not serve our interests to walk away from South Africa." Commenting on this and other manifestations of the Reagan administration's South African policy, one study observed:

In point of fact the Reagan Administration has done just the opposite. Almost from the outset administration officials acted to ease previously strained relations between the two countries. On March 15, 1981, UN Ambassador Jeane Kirkpatrick met in New York with South Africa's Chief of South African Military Intelligence and three of his aides. . . . While the administration has repeatedly and publicly expressed opposition to apartheid, it has otherwise isolated itself internationally. In August 1981 the United States voted against its Western allies in vetoing a UN Security Council resolution which strongly criticized South Africa for its incursion into Angola.[30]

The Reagan administration's continued opposition to strong UN action against Pretoria was demonstrated in October 1985 when it vetoed a proposal that would have required the Security Council to consider mandatory economic and political sanctions against the South African government if it failed to end apartheid, and then abstained in a vote on a resolution, subsequently adopted, urging governments to suspend new investments in South Africa.

The Reagan Administration's image as a foe of apartheid was not helped by other incidents in its early years. UN Ambassador Kirkpatrick, whose reception of the South African general was explained on the grounds that she did not realize the military character of the person with whom she was meeting, further alienated South African blacks by her attempt at a justification for U.S. sanctions against the Soviet Union but not against South Africa: "Marxism is more dangerous than racism."[31]

Among other pro-Pretoria moves by the Reagan administration in its first years in office were its endorsement of South Africa's controversial new constitution, which failed to extend political rights to blacks, and its issuance of a number of licenses: for the export of shock batons and for high technology sales, covering commodities with dual-use capabilities, including nuclear.

The Reagan administration's South African policy was frequently and harshly condemned by black African leaders, most notably Nobel Peace Prize winner Bishop Desmond Tutu. The bishop in October 1984 stated, "in my view, the Reagan Administration has done precious little to advance [our liberation] struggle. If anything, it has assisted in making the South African Government more intransigent." In December 1984 he accused the administration of practicing an "immoral, evil, and totally un-Christian collaboration with South African apartheid." In October 1985 he denounced President Reagan and British and West German leaders as "racists" because of their opposition to economic sanctions against South Africa and remarked that Reagan's failure to mention South Africa in his UN General Assembly speech "underlines what one has been suspecting—that for him we are just statistics . . . pawns in the East-West power game."[32]

Summary

Both the Carter and the Reagan administrations made frequent and clear statements declaring their opposition to South Africa's system of apartheid, but in both cases the implementation of this attitude was complicated by the presence in the foreign policy picture of strategic/ideological interests. Both administrations were aware of and influenced by South Africa's role as a partner in dealing with regional problems in southern Africa, and both were concerned with the real or perceived threat of spreading Communist influence in this region, though the anticommunism note was more prominent in the Reagan South African policy than in that of Carter.

Again, while both administrations were officially committed to seeking an end to apartheid, neither was inclined to support strong UN action directed against this system of racial segregation, depending on explanatory statements to dispel the notion that this country's voting record demonstrated support for apartheid.

While there were similarities in the relationship of the two administrations on the question of human rights in South Africa, centering on the apartheid issue, there were also differences. Carter's general image was one of toughness toward the South African government, whereas the Reagan administration's policy of constructive engagement created the impression that this administration was more tolerant of the Pretoria regime. Carter's approach, moreover, won for him the friendship of South African blacks, who were convinced that he was really on their side; they were equally convinced, however, that the Reagan administration was a collaborator with Pretoria in maintaining the system that held them in subjection.

A final difference between the two administrations was that, whereas the Carter administration appeared to be less outspokenly critical of the South African regime as the administration came to the end of its term in office, the Reagan administration's public denunciation of this regime became more strident in its later years.

SOUTH KOREA

The human rights situation confronting the Carter and Reagan administrations in South Korea was to a considerable degree a product of this country's history, and this history combined with South Korea's geographic position to give it high strategic importance to the United States. The strategic factor, in turn, became the dominant note in both administrations' policies, overriding human rights as a concern for both Carter and Reagan.

The South Korea with which Carter and Reagan dealt occupies part of a peninsula that had been annexed by Japan in 1910 then divided by World War II. The section north of the thirty-eighth parallel was occupied by Soviet troops and became one state, North Korea, under a Communist regime, with an estimated 1985 population of 20 million. The area south of the thirty-eighth parallel emerged as South Korea, politically organized under a republican constitution and having a 1985 population of 42 million.

The June 1950 invasion of South Korea by its neighbor to the north brought the United States into Korean affairs as an ally of South Korea in a war that ended in a stalemate. South Korea's resultant situation was described as "one of the most potentially severe imbalances in military power anywhere in the world."[33] This imbalance, judged to favor North Korea, created a security problem for South Korea, whose political leaders have consistently cited "the threat from the north" as justifying practices that have been widely condemned as violations of South Koreans' rights. This rationale has been challenged by those who point to Israel, for example, as evidence that the mere presence of an external threat is not sufficient reason for a government to run roughshod over the rights of its people.

The repressive practices inflicted on the people of South Korea were instituted by a succession of authoritarian regimes, the first of which, under Syngman Rhee, held power for twelve years. Rhee's resignation in April 1960, forced by a student-led uprising against his dictatorial rule, was followed by a brief period under what has been called "the only true democratic government South Korea has had since independence."[34] In May 1961 a military coup led by General Park Chung Hee began the second period of authoritarian rule since the Second World War. This era ended with the October 1979 assassination of Park by the Korean Central Intelligence Agency chief, Kim Jae Kyu, whose declared reason for this act was a desire to save the country from ruin and restore democracy.

Park's assassination paved the way for the coming to power of General Chun Doo Hwan, under whom, according to Donald L. Ranard, former director of the State Departments's Office of Korean Affairs, "the human rights situation in South Korea [was] no better than it was under Syngman Rhee."[35]

In South Korea Carter and Reagan thus saw a country where the human rights of the people had been abused by a succession of authoritarian regimes, a country described by Ranard as "synonymous with the struggle of a people for human dignity. Nowhere has this struggle been more persistent, more marked by courage and bravery and against greater adversities."[36]

They also saw a country that was closely linked with a number of American interests: (1) strategic, with South Korea seen as "the linchpin of the United States' strategic defense posture in Asia"; (2) political, with the objective of a democratic South Korea; (3) economic, with South Korea the ninth largest trading partner of the United States; and (4) cultural, as the United States sought to maintain connections with a country with a rich tradition in music, art, and literature.[37]

These interests provided the background for a policy vis-à-vis South Korea designed to serve the United States's overall objective of peace and stability in the Korean peninsula and in the larger Asian theater of which it was a part. The specific components of this policy were a number of actions and commitments that the United States undertook to ensure the independence of South Korea as a bulwark, hopefully democratic in nature, against Communist advances in the area. Thus, the United States was committed to defend South Korea in the event of an invasion of its territory. Extensive military and economic aid was provided that for some years was greater in volume than that which was extended to any other nation; American troops were stationed in South Korea, and South Korea was given diplomatic support by the United States.[38]

South Korea was thus seen and treated as a vital component in the overall pattern of U.S. political/security interests in that part of the globe, interests that demanded peace and stability in the Korean peninsula. In the opinion of at least some observers, however, peninsular peace and stability could be achieved only if South Korea were internally stable, and this stability, in turn, could prevail only if human rights were respected by this country's government. Congressman Lester L. Wolff made this point in 1980 hearings on U.S.–South Korean relations, when he insisted that "the U.S. position must continue to be that the best interests of the Korean people and the United States will be served by a return to progress toward restoring the democratic process." Agreeing with this position, Donald Ranard commented, "Without democratic institutions, without observance of recognized international standards of human rights, South Korea will remain an unstable country and a constant invitation to trouble in Asia."[39] The extent to which this conviction of the importance of human rights found expression in the South Korean policies of the Carter and Reagan administrations is the topic of this section.

The Carter Administration

As the Carter administration assumed office, it faced difficulties in its relations with South Korea because of Carter's emphasis on human rights and his commitment during his presidential campaign to withdraw American ground forces from this country. The administration was also quite conscious of the policy imperatives posed by American strategic needs and goals in the geographic area in which South Korea is located.

Carter's secretary of state, Cyrus Vance, expressed the policy problems created by these factors:

Given the importance of South Korea for the security of Japan and for our political and military position in East Asia, I recommended that we continue to press hard on [the human rights issue] but not to tie it to our economic or military assistance.

While the human rights situation in South Korea fell far short of what most of us felt was desirable, we constantly had to weigh the fact that only thirty-five miles to the north of Seoul was a nation in which control of the population was absolute and freedom non-existent. The contrast could not be ignored, and although some critics felt we were not vigorous enough in our advocacy of human rights in South Korea, I felt that a careful balance was essential, and made sure that it was maintained.[40]

The same awareness of the regional security factor appeared several years later, in remarks by Michael Armacost, deputy assistant secretary of state for East Asian and Pacific affairs. In the course of a congressional hearing he reminded his listeners that it was "important to remember that the context in which we view developments in Korea is dominated by our objective of insuring continuing peace and stability on the peninsula." The pursuit of this objective called for U.S. military support and other measures that could provide a deterrence against another outbreak of hostilities that could involve not only the two Koreas but China, the Soviet Union, Japan, and the United States.

Turning to the question of human rights in South Korea, Armacost observed that the threat of another invasion from the north had led to a "considerable emphasis in South Korea on maintaining stability through a fairly centralized political system." Because of this development in South Korea and the U.S. belief that political stability could exist only when democratic values prevailed, he continued, the U.S.–South Korean relationship was at times "troubled, despite the existence of very strong shared security interests."[41] It is apparent that the Carter administration and the South Korean leaders had opposite views of how domestic political stability was to be insured.

To summarize, the Carter administration's approach to South Korea was based on two premises: that the stability and the maintenance of the current strategic balance in northeastern Asia were items of "overwhelming interest" to the United States and that a broadly based South Korean government was important for the long-range stability and security of the peninsula. As another Carter administration official, Richard C. Holbrooke, noted, developing a policy based on these two premises was by no means easy, since they were not always "in total harmony." In his opinion, however, the handling of this task was made easier by the "exceptionally good cooperation" that prevailed between the State Department, the Defense Department, the White House staff, the command in Seoul and the embassy in Seoul, a "higher degree of coordination and cooperation than at any previous period over the last twenty years."

The Carter administration's handling of the policy problem of premises that were at times contradictory may also have been eased by another factor: an assumption that security considerations would receive higher priority. Thus, when asked whether there were any circumstances that would take precedence over such considerations, Holbrooke, speaking as assistant secretary of state for Asian and Pacific affairs, replied that he did not see "how one could consider the situation in Korea without taking the security situation into central account."[42]

The tendency to allow security considerations to outweigh human rights in policy decisions was reflected in the Carter administration's behavior in relation to Section 502B of the Foreign Assistance Act of 1961, as amended. Under this legislation, no security assistance was to be provided to any country whose government engaged in a consistent pattern of violations of internationally recognized human rights. Despite this prohibition and the poor human rights record of the South Korean regime, substantial U.S. military aid, ranging from $130 million to $276 million per year, was extended to this country throughout Carter's term in office. This high level of U.S. military aid expressed the administration's policy orientation as stated by Secretary Vance: a commitment to the principle that human rights concerns should influence security aid decisions, but also a determination to continue military aid to South Korea "for reasons of national security." In other words, human rights concerns would be given a hearing but would not control decisions in this policy area. At the same time, the Carter administration was acting within the law governing security aid by giving a legal justification for its actions in cases where human rights were an issue, the justification being the "exceptional national security considerations" provision in Section 502B.[43]

By elevating security considerations to the top place in the order of policy priorities, over human rights, the Carter administration attracted severe criticism from those who felt that he was not properly dealing with the human rights situation in South Korea. In the opinion of Donald Ranard, for example, Jimmy Carter was now

the latest of American Presidents to sacrifice human dignity on the altar of misperceived geopolitical factors or domestic political and economic considerations. Like his predecessors, Carter has failed to sufficiently comprehend that, hostile as it is, North Korea does not represent the main threat to the South. The chief threat comes from the political instability created by the lust for power of authoritarian rulers and the continual denial of the right of ordinary Koreans to participate in the democratic process.[44]

In another attack on the Carter administration's South Korean policy, Edwin M. Luidens of the National Council of Churches asserted in 1980:

Frustrations [of people seeking to enjoy their rights] can be doubled when it becomes clear that a human rights policy is being applied selectively: to those countries with which the United States is in tension, but not to countries with which we have close alliance.

Luidens continued with references to the consistency with which military and economic factors "override human rights in U.S. decision-making," a fact that was seen as putting this country in the same category as authoritarian regimes in this respect.[45] Another administration critic, J. Bryan Hehir, of the U.S. Catholic Conference, told a 1980 congressional subcommittee hearing:

U.S. policy in its present form reenforces [the] narrow view of security [as derived from military strength] rather than providing an alternative vision. The Carter policy has proven to be severely disappointing to the Koreans we saw. At the outset of this administration there was a conscious balance struck between human rights and security considerations in Korea . . . a welcome change from the Kissingerian style of ignoring human rights problems whenever the security question came into play. The Carter policy therefore aroused the hopes of the Korean people.

Today . . . the tension of the early years between human rights and security has been lost. Perhaps the cause of the shift is increased superpower tension; perhaps it is short-term election year tactics. Whatever the cause, the result is that U.S. policy . . . reenforces the direction of [South Korean leader] Chun Doo Hwan: security equals military security and human rights along with democratic institutions are dispensable items at this time.[46]

The reports on South Korea included in the Carter administration's annual surveys of human rights practices around the world also were subjected to negative criticisms. The 1979 report, for example, was accused of continuing "to accent whatever positive changes had taken place, while ignoring or glossing over continuing or worsening aspects of human rights violations," of containing distortions and expressing biases, of neglecting the area of economic/social rights, and of omitting important material, such as the abuses of the rights of groups of people.[47]

In the eyes of some critics, these alleged deficiencies in the administration's reports on South Korea revealed failures to establish reliable procedures to obtain accurate and complete information concerning the situation of human rights in South Korea. For example, it was said that the U.S. embassy in Seoul lacked senior officers with Korean language capability, limiting their ability to obtain accurate and objective information, that the embassy relied too much on the South Korean government for information, and that there was insufficient contact with the "lower" classes in South Korean society, with the result that U.S. personnel were not getting "the view from the bottom."[48]

The Carter administration was accused of having missed an opportunity to move South Korea in the direction of democracy in the period immediately following the assassination in 1979 of Park Chung Hee. South Koreans were quoted as saying that this period of time was "the last chance in modern history for the United States to show whether it would encourage those Koreans favoring a return to democratic processes or whether it would continue to show its racism by supporting repressive leadership on the grounds that the Koreans were not yet fit to govern themselves politically and determine their own destiny."[49]

This was the time, according to Donald Ranard,

when U.S. diplomacy should have been more insistent on progress toward democratic improvement. Our hesitation then only led to General Chun Doo Hwan immediately removing South Korean troops from the demilitarized zone and using them to seize the government in Seoul. The United States could have been more forceful in its reaction to what was in effect a most dangerous infraction of the chain of command since Park Chung Hee's 1961 coup.[50]

Several reasons were given for the alleged failure of the Carter administration to take pro-democratic action in the aftermath of the Park assassination. Pharis J. Harvey of the North American Coalition for Human Rights in Korea, asserting that Carter was not to be criticized for this turn of events, pointed to what he perceived to be "unresolved conflict within the administration," went on to point out that the State Department "was not forceful in pressing for political reform in Korea, and gave the lead to the Pentagon."[51]

Secretary of State Edmund Muskie cited several other factors when South Korean opposition leader Kim Dae Jung asked him why the United States "had not supported democracy" in his country at this critical time:

1. There was a fear in Washington that a tumultuous situation would ensue and that this would open the door to North Korea.
2. The administration was obsessed at this time with the Iranian hostage problem.
3. The South Korean crisis arose during a U.S. presidential year, and there was a consequent reluctance to take any controversial action that could be politically harmful.[52]

A final example of the kinds of negative criticism that the Carter administration received for its handling of the human rights situation in South

Korea is the administration's conduct at the time of the 1980 demonstrations at Kwangju against the martial law imposed by Chun Doo Hwan. Actions by paratroopers to suppress the demonstrations resulted in a civilian death toll of anywhere from 170 to 1,200. This event, in the opinion of one critic, should have led the administration to condemn the brutality at Kwangju severely or at least to cancel the scheduled visit to South Korea by the head of the U.S. Export-Import Bank. The visit subsequently took place, leading to an offer of increased credits for South Korea.[53]

At least one attempt was made on behalf of the Carter administration to assert that it had not been completely negligent in regard to the Kwangju incident. Deputy Assistant Secretary of State for Asian and Pacific Affairs Michael Armacost testified to a congressional subcommittee that "at the height of the disturbance at Kwangju, we publicly expressed the hope that when the situation had calmed, the Government would quickly resume a program of political development." In his testimony, Armacost also cited a number of actions by the Carter administration in the interests of human rights and democracy in South Korea:

1. Both publicly and privately expressed deep concern about actions taken by the South Korean martial law authorities.

2. Expressed concern about curbs on the political process, the placing of the National Assembly in limbo, the banning of political activity, the closing of universities, and the arrest of major political figures.

3. Postponed, and then did not reschedule, a visit to South Korea by a representative of the Overseas Private Investment Corporation.

4. Abstained on an Asian Development Bank loan for South Korea to develop the Inchon port.

This abstention, on human rights grounds, was not the only such action to be taken by the Carter administration in order to register its disapproval of South Korea's human rights record. From October 1977 through December 1980 seven such abstentions were recorded, five of them in the Asian Development Bank and the other two in the World Bank. In addition to these votes on proposed loans, the Carter administration responded to the abuses of human rights in South Korea by succeeding, in at least two cases, in delaying action in the Asian Development Bank on projected loans to this country.[54]

Also on the positive side of the Carter administration's response to the human rights situation in South Korea was the 1979 country report on human rights practices in this country. While the report is vulnerable to negative criticisms, it also called attention to abuses of human rights by South Korea's ruling regime. These violations included mistreatment of prisoners through torture, subjection to psychological pressures and beatings; serious undermining of the judicial system and the legal profession; invasion of the home; and restrictions on freedom of speech and press.

The 1979 annual report on human rights conditions in South Korea made frequent references to anti–human rights actions taken by the South Korean government under cover of the emergency decree then in effect. This decree—Emergency Measure No. 9—was cited by an administration spokesperson as one of the issues "over which we are most concerned," and this concern was "consistently made clear in our contacts with Korean Government officials at all levels." Carter himself made these contacts in a summer 1979 visit to South Korea, when he communicated his human rights concerns directly to South Korea's President Park as well as through other channels: the press; a joint communiqué; a toast, which was broadcast, at a state dinner; and meetings with church leaders and leaders of the National Assembly, including those in the opposition faction.[55]

Carter's meeting with opposition leaders in South Korea was another example of his administration's support for those who were trying to bring an end to their country's dominance by authoritarian regimes. Further evidence was what one observer called the administration's "intensified intervention" in the case of the most prominent opposition leader, Kim Dae Jung, on whose behalf the administration sought an open trial and a guarantee that he would not be executed.[56]

A final indication that the Carter administration did actively seek to lift the level of human rights observance in South Korea is the attitude of some South Korean government personnel toward Carter. One has asserted that "Carter was not popular with South Korea because of [his stand on] human rights." According to this official, Carter "abused South Korea in the name of human rights." This alleged punishment took the specific form of his threat to withdraw U.S. troops, which this official saw as an effort to "eliminate the fundamental basis for human rights," since the loss of American military support could mean the conquest of South Korea by its northern rival. "Without a country, there could be no human rights."[57]

The judgment on Carter that this South Korean governmental official expressed was, in short, that he ignored the security factor in his approach to human rights, an opinion that stands in direct opposition to the general view as to the place the Carter administration assigned to human rights vis-à-vis security concerns.

The Reagan Administration

As in other cases involving human rights situations, the Reagan administration's approach to the one in South Korea could be labeled "constructive engagement." This approach expressed two beliefs of the administration: (1) that quiet diplomacy was the tactic most likely to get results, and (2) that by enhancing the security relations between the two countries, the administration not only would be serving America's strategic interests but would be in a better position to have some influence over the South Korean government in human rights matters.

Reportedly, the Koreans appreciated the quiet diplomacy—defined by one administration official as "not saying anything unless we have something to say"—that the Reagan administration practiced. It was also seen as serving a useful function in individual cases, most notably the release of opposition leader Kim Dae Jung from a South Korean prison in 1982, whose release was attributed to a combination of Japanese and American pressure on the Korean government. Less spectacular, but certainly important, were U.S. Ambassador Richard Walker's "frequent" interventions on the private level on behalf of individuals.[58]

The Reagan administration's proclaimed preference for quiet diplomacy did not result in an avoidance of public statements on the subject of human rights in South Korea. In a November 1983 appearance before the South Korean National Assembly, for example, Reagan stressed his country's "welcome for the goals you have set for political democracy and increased respect for human rights." Again, a state dinner during the same visit to South Korea provided an opportunity for Reagan to state that "democracy and freedom of opinion are virtues the free world must cherish and defend"; and in what was reportedly the strongest human rights statement Reagan made during his stay in South Korea, he told a group of South Korean businessmen, academicians, human rights activists, and journalists that the United States "pays close attention to human rights in Korea not because we believe our security commitment gives us the right to intervene in your internal affairs but simply because such issues are at the center of our political ideology."[59]

Ambassador Walker also publicly expressed the administration's concern for human rights in South Korea in lectures and speeches in which he referred to the need for liberalization, pluralism, and resort to democratic processes in South Korea. By weaving these expressions into his addresses, the ambassador indirectly voiced his government's interest in the quality of his host country's domestic politics.[60]

The annual country reports on human rights practices constituted another channel through which the Reagan administration dealt publicly with the human rights situation in South Korea. In his comments on the preparation of the section on South Korea, an official in the State Department's Korean Office noted that this proceeded "without any pressure for change." This observation was made with special reference to the inclusion of material on the resort to torture in South Korea, an example of which was the report for 1985, where it was noted that the number of cases involving torture had "increased significantly" over the preceding year's statistics.

The report for 1985 also called attention to a number of other abuses of human rights in South Korea: the use of excessive force by the police; increased surveillance or house arrest of persons who are thought to have intentions of breaking the laws governing political dissent, as well as other misuse of the National Security Law in order to suppress dissent; less independence for the judiciary when the cases under consideration were politically sensitive; the practice of holding individuals as political prisoners; invasion of the privacy of the home; restrictions, sometimes severe, on the freedom of speech and press; the arrest or firing of teachers publishing criticisms of the government's education policy; and limitations on academic freedom and the freedom of peaceful assembly and association.

The Reagan administration's efforts to demonstrate a concern for human rights in South Korea failed to dispel the perception of this administration as a supporter of General Chun Doo Hwan, under whom the human rights situation in South Korea was said to be as bad as or worse than it was in the final stages of the Park regime. This perception is based on a record of administration actions that dates from the very beginning of its term in office. One was Reagan's reception of General Chun Doo Hwan, who had seized power in South Korea and had not yet been elected president under the new Korean constitution. Chun was the first head of state to be received by Reagan, and his prestige was considerably heightened as a result of this gesture. The move also served to create a bond between Chun and the new U.S. administration.

Reagan's visit to Seoul in November 1983 was a clear signal that his administration wanted to maintain the tie that it had established in 1980. As one report on this visit noted, this was the occasion for Reagan to "warmly embrace" the South Korean leader and assure him that "America is your friend and we are with you." The perception of Reagan's visit as an indication of his support for Chun was strengthened by his failure to express any outright criticism of the Chun regime's human rights record and by his remark to the National Assembly, that "the United States realizes how difficult political development is when, even as we speak, a shell from the North could destroy this Assembly." Commenting on this assembly appearance, one review of the Reagan administration's human rights record noted that "even as he spoke, Korean security forces were cracking down on political dissidents," something of which administration spokespersons claimed to be ignorant.[61]

The Reagan administration's attitude toward South Korean dissidents was another point of negative criticism of its approach to the human rights situation. Thus, while the administration could rightly claim some credit for the release from prison of Kim Dae Jung and his resulting freedom to take refuge in the United States, its attitude toward Kim when he announced his intention to return to South Korea early in 1985 was seen as less supportive. The State Department was reported to be opposed to Kim's return, "doing all it could to prevent it . . . for fear that [his return] would be disruptive." Particular criticism was directed at the Human Rights Bureau head Elliott Abrams for his position on the question of Kim's return, expressed in his statement that the United States "wanted to stay absolutely neutral" in the Kim case. In the opinion of one critic:

If he could not bring himself to advocate publicly Mr. Kim's right to participate in a democratic political system, Secretary Abrams should have restricted himself to the "quiet diplomacy" which the State Department says it employs with friendly countries on human rights questions. Instead, Secretary Abrams disparaged the threats to Mr. Kim's liberty already made by the South Korean Government and linked unrest in South Korea, motivated by severe restrictions on freedom, to North Korean designs.[62]

U.S. Ambassador Walker's conduct brought further reason to criticize the Reagan administration's attitude toward South Korea's political dissidents. In the opinion of one close observer of South Korean affairs, Walker had "no patience for the human rights forces in Korea" and a "contempt for the political opposition," which was shown in the fact that "he did not meet with opposition leaders." This alleged failure in the area of embassy contacts was said to extend to the South Korean human rights and religious communities, with whom there was "almost no dialogue."[63]

Negative criticism of the Reagan administration's handling of the human rights situation in South Korea extended to the quality of its reports on this situation, as contained in the State Department's annual review of human rights practices around the world. Thus, in their analysis of the report for 1984, the Americas and Helsinki Watches and the Lawyers Committee for International Human Rights found this report to be flawed at these points:

1. The section on freedom of peaceful assembly and association was described as "particularly inadequate" because of its "failure to mention the virtual destruction of every attempt to create independent unions" and the persecution of union leaders and members; its glossing over abusive treatment given women students; and its "lack of detail and analysis" in dealing with the government's handling of persons involved in demonstrations.

2. The section on freedom of religion, described as "similarly incomplete" and "overly optimistic," omitting to mention the repression of certain congregations.

3. Other alleged deficiencies include the "minimizing" of the problem of the methods used to break up demonstrations and meetings of various groups; the use of the term "allegations" in discussing instances of torture and other cruel, inhuman, or degrading treatment; and failure to mention the special "preventive custody centers" for use of political prisoners and others.[64]

A final functional area in which the Reagan administration's response to the South Korean human rights situation has been criticized is bilateral and multilateral assistance for this country. The Reagan administration, like its predecessor, gave a higher priority to security interests than human rights concerns in determining whether or not bilateral aid should be extended to South Korea. This approach exposed both administrations to the charge of failing to comply completely with Section 502B of the amended Foreign Assistance Act of 1961, designed to prevent grants of aid to countries with poor human rights records.

The criticism of the Reagan administration at the point of its alleged failure in relation to Section 502B centers on the accusation that, unlike Carter's, the Reagan administration failed to provide a "coherent legal basis" for its aid policies vis-à-vis South Korea. Instead, so the criticism goes, the Reagan administration sought to justify its aid policy by asserting that the extension of aid would encourage this country's regime to lift the level of its human rights observance. This claim was accompanied by an interpretation of the "consistent pattern of violations" clause under which a country that had made improvements in its human rights performance was held to be no longer guilty of "consistent" abuses. These arguments by the administration in support of its aid policy for Korea and other countries were rejected by critics as being "hard to reconcile with the letter or the spirit of what Congress had in mind when it adopted its human rights legislation."[65]

Finally, the Reagan administration was accused of failing to support the cause of human rights in South Korea through its reversal of the Carter administration's policy concerning loans to South Korea from multilateral development banks. The Carter administration used South Korea's poor human rights record as the grounds for refusing to support such loans to this country. From November 1983 through February 1985, however, the Reagan administration voted for sixteen loans to South Korea from the Asian Development Bank and the World Bank, the total value of which was $1,107 million.

Summary

The response of both administrations to the human rights situation in South Korea was to make some effort to induce this country's leaders to improve their performance, but to do so within a general policy framework that gave precedence to political/security considerations. "Security" in this instance was defined in relation to alleged external threats to South Korea's physical integrity, not to possible internal disruptions caused by popular rebellion against the repressive regimes in power. Both administrations thus rejected the argument that South Korea's true security depended on the establishment of a democratic political order that respected human rights, choosing instead to lend support to Korean rulers who were seen as useful in the American quest for peace and stability in the East Asian theater.

While both administrations thus followed a policy of support for oppressive South Korean regimes for geopolitical reasons, they differed in the way they put this policy into action. In extending security assistance to South Korea, both administrations violated national legislation that prohibited such aid in the case of countries guilty of human rights abuses, but only the Carter administration presented a legal justification for so doing: an appeal to the "extraordinary circumstances" loophole in the restrictive legislation. Again, while Carter refused to carry the policy of providing aid for South Korea to the point of supporting loans to this country by international financial institutions, the Reagan administration placed no such limit on U.S. assistance to the Koreans, reversing Carter's position concerning multilateral aid to them.

NOTES

1. Data given here are from William E. Smith, "Black Rage, White Fist," *Time*, August 5, 1985; *The World Almanac and Book of Facts, 1986* (New York: Newspaper Enterprise Association, Inc., 1985), p. 600; *The 1986 Information Please Almanac* (Boston: Houghton Mifflin, 1985), p. 260; and Randy Nunnelee, *South Africa and U.S. Policy* (Washington, D.C.: National Impact, August 1985).

2. *Everyman's United Nations*, 8th ed. (New York: United Nations, 1968), pp. 155–158; Opinion pages, *The New York Times*, August 11, 14, 1985; "U.S.–South African Trade," *World Press Review* (New York: Stanley Foundation, July 1985), p. 56; and *Human Rights: A Compilation of International Instruments* (New York: United Nations, 1983), p. 29.

3. Kevin Danaher, *In Whose Interest? A Guide to U.S.–South African Relations* (Washington, D.C.: Institute for Policy Studies, 1984), pp. 101–103.

4. Cyrus R. Vance, *Hard Choices: Critical Years in America's Foreign Policy* (New York: Simon and Schuster, 1983), p. 256.

5. Ibid., p. 257.

6. Clyde Ferguson and William R. Cotter, "South Africa: What Is to Be Done," *Foreign Affairs* 56 (October 1977-January 1978): 263.

7. Danaher, *In Whose Interest?*, p. 61.

8. David B. Ottoway, "Reagan Action Signals Reversal of Policy Toward South Africa," *The Washington Post*, September 11, 1985.

9. United Nations, *General Assembly Official Records*, 33rd Session, 93rd Plenary Meeting, January 24, 1979, pp. 122–124.

10. Ottoway, "Reagan Action Signals Reversal."

11. Conversations at the Department of State, October 1984.

12. United Nations, *General Assembly Official Records*, 32nd Session, 55th Plenary Meeting, November 22, 1978, p. 914.

13. Vance, *Hard Choices*, p. 265.

14. Zbigniew Brzezinski, *Power and Principle* (New York: Farrar, Straus, and Giroux, 1985), p. 55.

15. Conversations at the Department of State, October 1984.

16. Ibid., September 1985; Danaher, *In Whose Interest?*, pp. 80, 81; Chester A. Crocker, "South Africa: Strategy for Change," *Foreign Affairs* 59 (Winter 1980/1981): 326.

17. Danaher, *In Whose Interest?*, p. 81.

18. Lawrence S. Eagleburger, San Francisco address, June 23, 1983.

19. George Shultz, Washington, D.C. address, April 16, 1985, and Chester A. Crocker, San Francisco address, August 16, 1985.

20. U.S. Department of State, "The U.S. Response to Apartheid in South Africa," *Current Policy No. 688* (Washington, D.C.: U.S. Department of State, Bureau of Public Affairs, April 17, 1985), p. 2.

21. James McCartney, "Reagan Faces Choice on Apartheid," *The Centre Daily Times*, State College, Pa., August 25, 1985.

22. "The President's Sanctions Against South Africa," *The New York Times*, September 10, 1985.

23. Ottoway, "Reagan Action Signals Reversal"; and Sheila Rule, "American Envoy Back in Pretoria," *The New York Times*, September 11, 1985.

24. Bernard Weintraub, "U.S. Officials Bid South Africa Open Talk with Blacks," *The New York Times*, July 26, 1985.

25. Martin Tolchin, "U.S. Asks Pretoria to Lift its Decree on Special Powers," *The New York Times*, July 27, 1985.

26. Glenn Frankel, "U.S. Envoy Returns, Criticizes South Africa," *The Washington Post*, September 11, 1985.

27. Bernard Gwertzman, "State Department Denounces Pretoria," *The New York Times*, August 29, 1985.

28. Editorial, "Reagan's Word on Apartheid," *The Boston Globe*, December 15, 1985.

29. The preceding discussion is based on issues of *The New York Times*, *The Washington Post*, and *The Centre Daily Times* (State College, Pa.), passim.

30. Americas Watch, Helsinki Watch, Lawyers Committee for International Human Rights, *The Reagan Administration's Human Rights Policy: A Mid-Term Review* (New York and Washington, D.C.: Authors, 1982), pp. 42–43.

31. Americas Watch, Helsinki Watch, Lawyers Committee for International Human Rights, *Failure: The Reagan Administration's Human Rights Policy in 1983* (New York: Authors, 1984), p. 63.

32. Americas Watch, Helsinki Watch, Lawyers Committee for International Human Rights, *In the Face of Cruelty: The Reagan Administration's Human Rights Record in 1984* (New York: Authors, 1985), p. 79; Joan Mower, "Tutu Accuses U.S. of 'Immoral' Collaboration," *The Centre Daily Times*, State College, Pa., December 4, 1984; and Elaine Sciolino, "Tutu Denounces Reagan as Racist," *The New York Times*, October 29, 1985.

33. Paul D. Wolfowitz, assistant secretary of state for Asian/Pacific affairs, address in Arlington, Va., August 12, 1985.

34. Donald L. Ranchard, *Korea: Perspectives on a Flawed U.S. Policy*, International Policy Report (Washington, D.C.: Center for International Policy, February, 1983), p. 2.

35. Ibid.

36. Donald L. Ranard, in *The Congressional Record*, February 23, 1985 (S1905 Senate).

37. Ranard, *Korea: Perspectives*, p. 2.

38. Ibid.

39. Ibid, p. 3; and U.S. Congress, House of Representatives, Committee on Foreign Affairs, *United States–South Korean Relations*, *Hearings Before the Subcommittee on*

Asian and Pacific Affairs, 96th Cong., 2d Sess., June 25, August 28, 1980 (Washington, D.C.: U.S. Government Printing Office, 1980), p. 2.

40. Cyrus R. Vance, *Hard Choices: Critical Years in America's Foreign Policy* (New York: Simon and Schuster, 1983), pp. 32, 127.

41. U.S. Congress, *United States–South Korean Relations*, p. 34.

42. Ibid., pp. 28, 30.

43. International League for Human Rights and the International Human Rights Law Group, *Democracy in South Korea: A Promise Unfulfilled: Report on Human Rights, 1980–1985* (New York: Authors, 1985), pp. 98, 100, 101.

44. U.S. Congress, House of Representatives, Committee on Foreign Affairs, *Human Rights in Asia: Non-Communist Countries: Hearings Before the Subcommittee on Asian and Pacific Affairs and on International Organizations*, 96th Cong., 2d Sess., February 4, 6, 7, 1980 (Washington, D.C.: U.S. Government Printing Office, 1980), pp. 333–334.

45. Ibid., pp. 100, 101.

46. U.S. Congress, *United States–South Korean Relations*, pp. 56, 57.

47. Pharis Harvey, *Human Rights in South Korea*, Current Issues (Washington, D.C.: Center for International Policy, 1980), p. 5; and U.S. Congress, *Human Rights in Asia: Non-Communist Countries*, p. 107.

48. U.S. Congress, *Human Rights in Asia: Non-Communist Countries*, pp. 98–99, 186–187.

49. Ibid., p. 100.

50. Ranard, *Korea: Perspectives*, p. 3.

51. Pharis J. Harvey, conversation with the author, Washington, D.C., May 1985.

52. Ibid.

53. Ranard, *Korea: Perspectives*, p. 3, and *Democracy in South Korea*, pp. 28–29.

54. U.S. Congress, *United States–South Korean Relations*, pp. 5–6, 10, 16–17, and *Democracy in South Korea*, p. 105.

55. U.S. Congress, House of Representatives, Committee on Foreign Affairs, *Human Rights and U.S. Foreign Policy: Hearings Before the Subcommittee on International Organizations*, 96th Cong., 1st Sess., May 2 and 10; June 21; July 12; and August 2, 1979, (Washington, D.C.: U.S. Government Printing Office, 1979), p. 472.

56. J. Bryan Hehir, in U.S. Congress, *United States–South Korean Relations*, pp. 57–58.

57. Conversation at the South Korean Embassy, May 1985.

58. Conversations with representatives of nongovernmental organizations and at the Department of State, October 1984 and May 1985, and *Democracy in South Korea*, p. 135.

59. *Failure*, pp. 67–69.

60. Conversations with nongovernmental organizations' personnel, May 1985.

61. Ibid.; *Democracy in South Korea*, pp. 113, 133–135; and *Failure*, pp. 67–68.

62. Conversations at the Department of State, May 1985; and *In the Face of Cruelty*, pp. 88, 89.

63. Conversations at the Department of State, May 1985.

64. Americas Watch, Helsinki Watch, Lawyers Committee for International Human Rights, *Critique: Review of the Department of State's Country Reports on Human Rights Practices for 1984* (New York: Authors, 1985), pp. 90–94.

65. *Democracy in South Korea*, pp. 102, 103.

Conclusions

This study has presented a number of similarities and differences in the human rights policies of the Carter and Reagan administrations. The similarities, summarized below, indicate a high degree of continuity in U.S. human rights foreign policy.

1. A general orientation that placed human rights within the context of broad, overall foreign policy interests and demands with human rights subordinate to national political/security interests with an assertion of the compatibility of the two areas of foreign policy concern.

2. A mixture of humanitarianism and pragmatism in the rationale for a human rights policy.

3. A readiness to take advantage of loopholes in national human rights laws in order to extend aid to countries with poor human rights records, for political/security reasons.

4. A susceptibility to congressional influence concerning human rights policy in the forms of legislation, pressure to act, and support for pro–human rights actions and procedures.

5. A willingness to use all available tactics to implement policy: quiet and open diplomacy, pressure and inducements, bilateral and multilateral aid programs, careful preparation of annual reports on human rights practices of other countries, and promotion of democracy and democratic institutions abroad.

The differences between the Carter and Reagan human rights policies emphasize the significance of the identity of the person who occupies the presidency. In summary, these differences are:

1. While both administrations were officially committed to human rights, this commitment was stronger and more consistently present in the Carter administration

than in that of Reagan, whose support for human rights at times developed only as a result of pressures from domestic sources and developments in other countries.

2. While both administrations related human rights to the East–West political conflict, anticommunism dominated Reagan's foreign, and hence human rights policy to a greater extent than it did Carter's. Reagan's human rights policy consequently was less evenhanded and credible than Carter's.

3. Because of its inclusion of economic/social rights, Carter's definition of human rights was more comprehensive and more in conformity with international human rights law than Reagan's.

4. Carter was more active in seeking to extend U.S. human rights policy into the area of adherence to international human rights conventions and covenants.

5. While Carter began his tenure by displaying a determination to establish and implement a human rights policy, even to the point of precipitating conflict with the foreign policy bureaucracy, Reagan's first moves indicated an indifference if not hostility to human rights: a difference whose significance derives at least in part from the assumption that an executive's first actions are the most reliable indicators of his attitudes and priorities.

6. Carter made greater use of the procedures of international financial institutions to express concern for human rights situations than did Reagan, who, with some later exceptions, tended to resort to this tactic mainly when loans to leftist governments were being considered.

Several conclusions may be drawn from these comparisons, the first of which concerns the question: Which administration was more supportive of human rights? Answers to this question clearly reflect value judgments on a number of key points concerning the human rights performance of the two administrations, one of which is the tactics they employed to implement their policies. It is true that both administrations used the same set of tactics, but they differed in the emphasis they gave to particular techniques, a fact that opens the door to dispute as to which administration's tactical preferences better served the cause of human rights.

Also in the area of value judgments is the problem of the impression each president created concerning his determination to advance the cause of human rights. In a policy area like this, impression, or image, is of real significance: it affects the credibility that leaders of foreign governments attach to the human rights representations of a particular American president, and it affects the seriousness with which administrative personnel take the professed human rights commitment of a particular president.

The impression left with this author, from all the material and considerations in this book, is that in Carter there was a stronger commitment to human rights than in his successor, a judgment that will seem obvious to some observers, doubtful to others, and erroneous to still others. There will also be mixed reactions to the author's conclusion that the comparisons between the two administrations construct a picture of Carter as a true leader in the field of human rights, with Reagan emerging as a reluctant, less effective proponent. This conclusion is presented in full recognition of the fact that it is very difficult to compare the relative contributions to a cause such as human rights made by a ground-breaking president and one who comes on the scene after the initial spade work has been done.

A second conclusion to be reached from comparing the two administrations is that no administration can be expected to be completely supportive of human rights, making no compromises with political/security or other concerns, nor is any administration likely to be totally indifferent or hostile to human rights. A thoroughgoing consistency in either direction, in other words, is not to be sought.

A third conclusion to be drawn from this study has to do with the place of human rights in U.S. foreign policy, and several observations may be made on this point:

1. The presence, to one extent or another, of human rights in the foreign policies of two successive administrations, representing opposing political parties, with chief executives entering office with different degrees of official commitment to human rights suggests the durability of human rights as a foreign policy element. While the survival of this component through one change in administrations is no guarantee, in itself, of this element's permanence, it does lend support to the assumption that human rights has been established as a member of this country's family of foreign policy concerns.

2. The durability of human rights as a foreign policy element is further suggested by the evidence, in the experience of two administrations, that this policy factor has been institutionalized within the American political system. This process has occurred within the executive branch and its supporting foreign service establishment as a result of several factors: (1) the successful fight by the Carter administration to win a place for human rights in the foreign policy decision-making process, (2) some years of experience in including human rights in this process, and (3) largely through congressional initiatives, the including of human rights personnel at various levels of the State Department's structure and the involving of U.S. embassy personnel in the whole human rights picture, mainly through the preparation of the mandated annual country reports on human rights practices.

   The institutionalization of human rights has also occurred within the legislative branch, with its subcommittees responsible for the oversight of the substantial body of human rights laws enacted by Congress, and this legislation itself constitutes an additional and most significant form of institutionalization. The fact and influence of the institutionalization of human rights in and through the legislative branch were clearly evident in the experience of both administrations.

3. It is not enough, however, for human rights merely to survive as a foreign policy element: To be of any significance as such, it must be an active, positive concern, one that is truly a part of the interaction between the American and other governments. The experience of two administrations indicates that human rights is not only a surviving but an active foreign policy element. Thus, while both

administrations subordinated human rights to political/security concerns, this subordination did not mean exclusion, for both administrations raised the human rights issue vis-à-vis abusive governments even while granting them material aid, for strategic reasons.

Human rights has thus become not only an established part of the foreign policy process, but one that has been an active element in this country's relations with other nations. Whether or not this is a desirable development is another matter, and this is the subject of the final conclusion to this study. Here the question is, have the human rights policies of these administrations produced results that justify the continued inclusion of this issue in U.S. foreign policy?

This is obviously a most difficult question to answer. It is impossible, for example, to determine how many cases of violations have been prevented because certain regimes have known that the U.S. government is actively concerned with the level of their human rights performance. It is also impossible to say with absolute certainty that improvements that have occurred in particular situations after an expression of American concern were the result of this expression or of some other factor(s). Again, there is a philosophical element involved in this matter of evaluating a human rights policy: how many identifiable cases of human rights successes, such as the release of prisoners, are necessary in order to justify this policy? Then, too, the question arises as to whether the policy is to be judged strictly on the basis of immediate, recognizable "successes" in dealing with particular situations, or whether consideration should also be given to the possible long-term, "deferred dividends" impact of the policy. And finally, what weight is to be given to such intangible, yet politically significant factors as the image projected abroad of a United States that is not only a superpower but one that cares about the conditions under which people in other countries live?

While the question of the effectiveness of the human rights policies of the Carter and Reagan administrations is undoubtedly hard to answer, some claims have been made on behalf of these efforts that deserve a hearing. Thus various spokespersons for these administrations have asserted that:

1. Pressures brought on the issue of disappearances helped decrease the number of such occurrences in Argentina and Chile.

2. The number of instances of torture around the world has been reduced.

3. Some governments have become more democratic, there have been more free elections, and press censorship has decreased. Pro-democratization contacts were made with the military, for example, in Argentina and Uruguay.

4. Significant numbers of prisoners were released in various countries, for example, Peru, Indonesia, and five African nations: Guinea, Niger, Rwanda, Swaziland, and Sudan.

5. Important public opinion sectors in various countries have moved to a pro–United

States position. This switch has occurred among labor, trade unions, intellectuals, and students.

6. Some easing of repression was accomplished, as, for example, in the Philippines under Marcos, and in the successful pressure exerted on El Salvador in regard to death squads.

7. Support has been provided for human rights activists and political opponents of oppressive regimes; the survival of South Korean opposition leader, Kim Dae Jung, for example, was attributed to U.S. support. Public indications of U.S. backing for some dissident groups shielded them from repressive measures. Human rights groups in various countries became bolder, and the loneliness of victims of oppression was somewhat eased.

8. The work of such international agencies as the UN and OAS Commissions on Human Rights was strengthened.

9. The level of human rights consciousness around the world was lifted, and the place of human rights as an item for discussion among diplomats enhanced.

10. The political image of the United States was improved as it became more active as a moral force.

Much of this testimony would, of course, fail to qualify as "hard evidence" of the effectiveness of the human rights efforts of two successive U.S. administrations. This fact, however, does not destroy the value of these representations as indications that this country's human rights policy has made a positive contribution to bettering life around the world. This author, for one, is satisfied that the record of accomplishments established by two administrations more than justifies the retention of human rights as a high priority element in this country's foreign policy.

This writer is also of the opinion that the justification for a human rights policy is not the number of successes it achieves, since the success of any human rights effort depends on many factors that are beyond this nation's control. The justification, rather, lies in the fact that the United States is the kind of country it is in regard to political and moral values. Consequently, it is not only appropriate but necessary for all American administrations to make every effort to see that people everywhere have an opportunity to enjoy the highest possible quality of life. And this effort can be made through a well-formulated and aggressively implemented human rights policy.

Bibliography

ADDRESSES

Abrams, Elliott. "Human Rights Policy." Georgetown University, Washington, D.C., October 12, 1983. U.S. Department of State, Bureau of Public Affairs, Selected Documents Series no. 22, December 1983.

Derian, Patricia. "U.S. Commitment to Human Rights." Milwaukee, Wisc., June 13, 1980. U.S. Department of State, Bureau of Public Affairs, Current Policy Series no. 198, June 13, 1980.

Eagleburger, Lawrence S. "Southern Africa: America's Responsibility for Peace and Change." San Francisco, June 23, 1983. U.S. Department of State, Bureau of Public Affairs, Current Policy Series no. 497, June 23, 1983.

Evans, Gareth. "The Australian Approach to Human Rights." United Nations Commission on Human Rights, Geneva, Switzerland, February 8, 1985. New York: Australian Information Service.

Mitterand, François. Address, 65th Congress of the League for the Rights of Man, Paris, April 20, 1985.

Muskie, Edmund S. "The Foreign Policy of Human Rights." University of Wisconsin at Milwaukee, October 21, 1980. U.S. Department of State, Bureau of Public Affairs, Current Policy Series no. 241, October 21, 1980.

Shultz, George P. "Human Rights and the Moral Dimension of U.S. Foreign Policy." Peoria, Ill., February 22, 1984. U.S. Department of State, Bureau of Public Affairs, Current Policy Series no. 551, February 22, 1984.

Thyden, James. "Ethnic Diplomacy, Human Rights, and Foreign Policy." Chicago, Ill., speaker's manuscript.

Wolfowitz, Paul D. "Recent Security Developments in Korea." Arlington, Va., August 12, 1985. Department of State, Bureau of Public Affairs, Current Policy Series no. 731, August 1985.

ARTICLES

Carleton, David, and Michael Stohl. "The Foreign Policy of Human Rights: Rhetoric and Reality from Jimmy Carter to Ronald Reagan." *Human Rights Quarterly* 7, no. 2 (May 1985).

Cohen, Stephen B. "Conditioning U.S. Security Assistance on Human Rights Practices." *American Journal of International Law* 76, no. 2 (April 1982).

Crocker, Chester A. "South Africa: Strategy for Change." *Foreign Affairs* 59, no. 2 (Winter 1980/1981).

Ferguson, Clyde, and William R. Cotter. "South Africa: What Is to Be Done?" *Foreign Affairs* 56 (October 1977–January 1978).

Nolan, Cathal J. "The Influence of Parliament on Human Rights in Canadian Foreign Policy." *Human Rights Quarterly* 7, no. 3 (August 1985).

BOOKS AND BROCHURES

Americas Watch, Helsinki Watch, Lawyers Committee for International Human Rights. *Critique: Review of the Department of State's Country Reports on Human Rights Practices for 1984*. New York: Authors, 1985.

————. *Failure: The Reagan Administration's Human Rights Policy in 1983*. New York: Authors, 1984.

————. *In the Face of Cruelty: The Reagan Administration's Human Rights Record in 1984*. New York and Washington, D.C.: Authors, 1985.

————. *The Reagan Administration's Human Rights Policy: A Mid-Term Review*. New York and Washington, D.C.: Authors, 1982.

Atwood, Brian. *Plain Talk on Human Rights*. Current Issues. Washington, D.C.: Center for International Policy, 1981.

Brown, Cynthia, ed. *With Friends Like These*. The Americas Watch Report on Human Rights and U.S. Policy in Latin America. New York: Pantheon Books, 1985.

Brzezinski, Zbigniew. *Power and Principle*, rev. ed. New York: Farrar, Straus, and Giroux, 1985.

Carter, Jimmy. *A Government As Good As Its People*. New York: Simon and Schuster, 1977.

————. *Keeping Faith: Memoirs of a President*. New York: Bantam Books, 1982.

————. *Why Not the Best?* New York: Bantam Books, 1976.

Cook, Thomas I., and Malcolm Moos. *Power Through Purpose: The Realism of Idealism*. Baltimore, Md.: Johns Hopkins University Press, 1954.

Danaher, Kevin. *In Whose Interest? A Guide to U.S.-South African Relations*. Washington, D.C.: Institute for Policy Studies, 1984.

Forsythe, David P., ed. *American Foreign Policy in an Uncertain World*. Lincoln: University of Nebraska Press, 1984.

Graebner, Norman A. *Ideas and Diplomacy: Readings in the Intellectual Tradition of American Foreign Policy*. New York: Oxford University Press, 1964.

Halperin, Morton H., and Arnold Kanter. *Readings in American Foreign Policy: A Bureaucratic Perspective*. Boston: Little, Brown, 1973.

Heaps, David. *Human Rights and U.S. Foreign Policy: The First Decade, 1973–1983*. New York: American Association for the International Commission of Jurists, 1984.

International League for Human Rights and International Human Rights Law Group. *Democracy in South Korea: A Promise Unfulfilled: Report on Human Rights 1980–1985*. New York: International League for Human Rights, 1985.

Irish, Marian, and Elke Frank. *U.S. Foreign Policy: Context, Conduct, and Content*. New York: Harcourt, Brace, Jovanovich, 1975.

Klare, Michael T., and Cynthia Arnson. *Supplying Repression: U.S. Support for Authoritarian Regimes Abroad*, rev. ed. Washington, D.C.: Institute for Policy Studies, 1981.

Kucharsky, David. *The Man from Plains*. New York: Harper and Row, 1976.

Lawyers Committee for Human Rights, the Watch Committees. *The Reagan Administration's Record on Human Rights in 1985*. New York and Washington, D.C.: Author, 1986.

Mazlish, Bruce, and Edwin Diamond. *Jimmy Carter: A Character Portrait*. New York: Simon and Schuster, 1979.

Morrell, Jim. *Achievement of the 1970s: U.S. Human Rights Law and Policy*. International Policy Report. Washington, D.C.: Center for International Policy, 1981.

Mower, A. Glenn, Jr. *The United States, the United Nations, and Human Rights*. Westport, Conn.: Greenwood Press, 1979.

National Impact. *South Africa and U.S. Policy*. Washington, D.C.: Author, 1985.

The 1986 Information Please Almanac. Boston: Houghton Mifflin, 1986.

Oye, Kenneth A., Donald Rothchild, and Robert J. Lieber, eds. *Eagle Entangled: U.S. Foreign Policy in a Complex World*. New York: Longman, 1979.

Padelford, Norman J., George A. Lincoln, and Lee D. Olvey. *The Dynamics of International Politics*, 3d ed. New York: Macmillan, 1976.

Ranard, Donald L. *Korea: Perspectives on a Flawed U.S. Policy*, International Policy Report. Washington, D.C.: Center for International Policy, 1983.

Rossiter, Caleb. *The Financial Hit List*. International Policy Report. Washington, D.C.: Center for International Policy, 1984.

————. *Human Rights: The Carter Record, the Reagan Reaction*. International Policy Report. Washington, D.C.: Center for International Policy, 1984.

U.S. Department of State, Bureau of Public Affairs. *Southern Africa: Constructive Engagement*. Washington, D.C.: U.S. Government Printing Office, 1985.

The World Almanac and Book of Facts 1986. New York: Newspaper Enterprise Association, 1986.

DOCUMENTS

France. *Human Rights and French Foreign Policy*, Documents from France, vol. 16.85. Washington, D.C.: French Embassy and Press Service, 1985.

National Advisory Council on International Monetary and Financial Policies. *International Finance: Annual Report to the President and to the Congress*. Washington, D.C.: U.S. Government Printing Office, various editions.

Norway, Royal Ministry and Foreign Affairs. *Norway and the International Protection of Human Rights*. Sorting No. 93, April 22, 1977.

United Nations. *Human Rights: A Compilation of International Instruments*. New York: United Nations, 1983.

————. *Official Records*. United Nations General Assembly, Plenary Meetings, 33d Session, 93d Plenary Meeting, January 24, 1979, and 32d Session, 55th Plenary Meeting, November 22, 1973. New York: United Nations.

U.S. Congress, House of Representatives, Committee on Foreign Affairs. *Human Rights and U.S. Foreign Policy: Hearings Before the Subcommittee on International Organizations*. 96th Cong., 1st Sess., May 2 and 10, July 12, August 2, 1979. Washington, D.C.: U.S. Government Printing Office, 1979.

————. *Human Rights: Compilation of Documents Pertaining to Human Rights.* Washington, D.C.: U.S. Government Printing Office, 1983.

————. *Human Rights in Asia: Communist Countries: Hearing Before the Subcommittees on Asian and Pacific Affairs and on International Organizations.* 96th Cong., 2d Sess., October 1, 1980. Washington, D.C.: U.S. Government Printing Office, 1980.

————. *Human Rights in Asia: Non-Communist Countries: Hearings Before the Subcommittees on Asian and Pacific Affairs and on International Organizations.* 96th Cong., 2d Sess., February 4, 6, 7, 1980. Washington, D.C.: U.S. Government Printing Office, 1980.

————. *Human Rights in the Philippines: Hearing Before the Subcommittee on Human Rights and International Organizations.* 98th Cong., 1st Sess., September 22, 1983. Washington, D.C.: U.S. Government Printing Office, 1983.

————. *The Phenomenon of Torture: Hearings and Markup Before the Committee on Foreign Affairs and the Subcommittee on Human Rights and International Organizations.* 98th Cong., 2d Sess., May 15 and 16, September 6, 1984. Washington, D.C.: U.S. Government Printing Office, 1984.

————. *Political Killings by Governments of Their Citizens: Hearings Before the Subcommittee on Human Rights and International Organizations.* 98th Cong., 1st Sess., November 16 and 17, 1983. Washington, D.C.: U.S. Government Printing Office, 1983.

————. *Religious Persecution of the Baha'is in Iran: Hearing Before the Subcommittee on Human Rights and International Organizations.* 98th Cong., 2d Sess., May 2, 1984. Washington, D.C.: U.S. Government Printing Office, 1984.

————. *Review of U.S. Human Rights Policy: Hearings Before the Subcommittee on Human Rights and International Organizations.* 98th Cong., 1st Sess., March 3, June 28, September 21, 1983. Washington, D.C.: U.S. Government Printing Office, 1983.

————. *United States-South Korean Relations: Hearings Before the Subcommittee on Asian and Pacific Affairs.* 96th Cong., 2d Sess., June 25, August 28, 1980. Washington, D.C.: U.S. Government Printing Office, 1980.

U.S. Congress, House of Representatives, Committee on Foreign Affairs and Committee on Banking, Finance, and Urban Affairs. *Human Rights at the Multilateral Development Banks: Joint Hearing Before the Subcommittee on International Development Institutions and Finance and the Subcommittee on Africa.* 98th Cong., 1st Sess., June 22, 1983. Washington, D.C.: U.S. Government Printing Office, 1983.

U.S. Department of State. *Country Reports on Human Rights Practices for 1982: Report Submitted to the Committee on Foreign Affairs, House of Representatives, and to the Committee on Foreign Relations, Senate.* Washington, D.C.: U.S. Government Printing Office, 1983. Also reports for 1981 (1982), for 1983 (1984).

INTERVIEWS

Center for International Policy, Washington, D.C.
Department of Justice
Department of State
Department of the Treasury

Derian, Patricia, former Assistant Secretary of State for Human Rights and Humanitarian Affairs

Embassy of the Republic of South Africa to the United States

Embassy of the Republic of South Korea to the United States

Feinberg, Richard E., Overseas Development Council, Washington, D.C.

International Human Rights Law Group, Washington, D.C.

Schneider, Mark, former Deputy Assistant Secretary of State for Human Rights and Humanitarian Affairs

Zak, Marilyn, Washington, D.C., concerning the Agency for International Development

Index

About the Author

A. GLENN MOWER, JR. is Professor Emeritus of Political Science at Hanover College, Indiana. He is the author of *The United States, the United Nations, and Human Rights*, *The European Community and Latin America*, and *International Cooperation for Social Justice* (Greenwood Press 1979, 1982, 1985) in addition to numerous contributions to various professional journals.